Games for Vocabulary Practice

Interactive vocabulary
activities for all levels

Felicity O'Dell
and Katie Head

CAMBRIDGE
UNIVERSITY PRESS

CAMBRIDGE UNIVERSITY PRESS
Cambridge, New York, Melbourne, Madrid, Cape Town,
Singapore, São Paulo, Delhi, Mexico City

Cambridge University Press
The Edinburgh Building, Cambridge CB2 8RU, UK

www.cambridge.org
Information on this title: www.cambridge.org/9780521006514

First published 2003
13th printing 2013

Printed in Poland by Opolgraf

A catalogue record for this publication is available from the British Library

ISBN 978-0-521-00651-4 Paperback

Contents

Introduction

What roles can games play in vocabulary learning?

Researchers say that vocabulary must be encountered at least seven times before it is truly learnt. They also advise that words are most easily learnt when students manipulate them and make them their own in some memorable way. For both these reasons, games have a particularly important role to play in vocabulary learning: they provide an enjoyable way of revisiting words and they give students the opportunity to use them in a memorable context.

The activities suggested in this book are, thus, not intended to teach sets of completely new vocabulary: that would make the games far too difficult. Rather the activities are intended to help students consolidate their knowledge of English vocabulary.

How is the book organised?

There are 18 topic-based units in this book. Each unit has three games, one at each of three levels – elementary, intermediate and upper-intermediate to advanced. There is a map of the book, which gives a clear overview of the topics of the units, the vocabulary focus, activity types and student interaction patterns used in each of the 54 games in the book.

How is each game arranged?

Each activity consists of two pages: a page of notes for the teacher and a photocopiable page that may be freely duplicated for students. The teacher's notes on the left-hand pages provide you with information about:

Time

Aim

Materials

Key vocabulary

Warm-up

Main activity

Variation

Follow-up

Homework

The **Time** allocated for each activity is usually 40–45 minutes, though some activities are shorter. The suggested times include a warm-up activity and some follow-up work in the classroom. The teacher can, of course, make the games fit into a shorter lesson by omitting the warm-up or follow-up activities, or by doing them in different lessons.

The **Aim** for each activity clearly summarises the kind of language to be focused on.

The **Materials** section lists everything that will be required for the activity. It is assumed that students have pens and paper.

Key vocabulary lists the vocabulary that is required for the game. It is important that teachers should read through this section when deciding whether a game is appropriate for a particular group of learners.

The **Warm-up** section suggests ways of familiarising the students with the language which will be required in the activity. Depending on the level of the class, you may need to spend longer on this part of the lesson – though with stronger groups you may need to spend little or no time on this section.

The **Main activity** section explains the steps of the activity as clearly and concisely as possible. We would recommend in most cases that you demonstrate these steps to the students instead of just reading them out to them. In some cases you may feel it would be helpful to note down the key steps on the classroom board.

The **Variation** section suggests ways of adapting the basic game for different classroom situations or contexts. Occasionally there are suggestions for a completely different game, but still using the same photocopiable materials.

The **Follow-up** section suggests optional classroom activities to develop and practise further the language worked with in the games. These follow-up activities may be used in a later lesson, if that is more appropriate, or they may be omitted.

The **Homework** section provides a couple of different suggestions for homework tasks based on the work of the activity. These tasks are, of course, optional but we strongly recommend that you choose one of them for your students, in order to help them learn the key vocabulary more effectively.

What about the photocopiable materials?

The materials on the right-hand pages can be freely photocopied. Quite often you will also have to cut up the materials into separate cards, as indicated by the cutting lines. If you are lucky enough to have access to a laminator, we would recommend preparing laminated sets of materials so that they can be easily reused.

Learning from others

In some activities you will also see an acknowledgement. This is because many of the games we have used in this book have been learnt from or inspired by other people or by popular or traditional games that we know.

We hope that, just as we have adapted games we learnt from others, you will do the same with the activities we present here. We feel sure that many of the photocopiable materials we offer here can be used in different ways from those we have suggested. Similarly, many of the activities described can be used with a different vocabulary focus to meet the needs of different groups. We hope that you will find lots of interesting ways in which you can adapt and be creative with the activities in this book.

Above all, we very much hope that your students will enjoy playing these games and that they will also help them to consolidate their knowledge of English vocabulary.

Felicity O'Dell and Katie Head

Games for Vocabulary Practice

Map of the book

Map of the book

Activity	Level	Vocabulary focus	Activity type	Student interaction	Time (minutes)	Page
UNIT 14 The world of work						
14.1 Who, where and what?	Elementary	Jobs and workplace	Card game	Pairs	30–35	90
14.2 Guess my job	Intermediate	Jobs and describing them	Yes/no questions	Whole class	35–40	92
14.3 Dangerous and stressful jobs	Upper-intermediate to advanced	Jobs and why they are dangerous or stressful	Categorising and ranking	Groups of 3–4	40–45	94
UNIT 15 Money and shopping						
15.1 Bring and buy sale	Elementary	Prices, buying and selling	Role play	Whole class	40–45	96
15.2 Crossword conversations	Intermediate	Money and shopping, and defining language	Crosswords and defining	Pairs	40–45	98
15.3 Get rich quick quiz	Upper-intermediate to advanced	Idioms and language connected with money	Quiz	Groups of 2–3	35–45	100
UNIT 16 Past experiences						
16.1 Past time dominoes	Elementary	Past time expressions	Four-sided dominoes	Groups of 3	35–40	102
16.2 Phrasal verbs auction	Intermediate	Phrasal verbs in sentences about the past	Auction of correct and incorrect sentences	Pairs	40–45	104
16.3 What a great story!	Upper-intermediate to advanced	Language for describing and reviewing a film or book	Categorising words and writing a film summary	Groups of 3–4	40–45	106
UNIT 17 Science and technology						
17.1 A day in the modern office	Elementary	The modern office and computers	Spot the difference	Pairs	40–45	108
17.2 Sci-tech board game	Intermediate	Names of inventions, sciences, scientists, planets and man-made objects	Board game	Groups of 4–5	35–45	110
17.3 Definitions	Upper-intermediate to advanced	Modern concepts in computers, entertainment, work, transport and science	Define and guess	Whole class or groups of 6–10	30–40	112
UNIT 18 Social and environmental issues						
18.1 Find five	Elementary	The natural world	Grid completion	Individually, then in pairs	35–45	114
18.2 Social survey	Intermediate	Social issues	Survey and discussion	Individually, then in groups of 3–4	30–35	116
18.3 Compounds	Upper-intermediate to advanced	Compound nouns of social and environmental issues	Card game	Groups of 3–4	35–45	118

1.1

All in a day

Level

Elementary

Time

40–45 minutes

Aim

To practise everyday expressions formed with the verbs *do, get, go, have, make* and *take*

Materials

For Warm-up, one copy of the Vocabulary grid for each student

One copy of the board for each group of three to four students

One dice for each group of three to four students

One counter (or equivalent) for each student

For Follow-up, a picture of a person that the students will all be able to see

Key vocabulary

do: the cleaning, the cooking, the ironing, the washing-up, your homework

get: cold, dressed, angry, tired

go: clubbing, running, shopping, swimming, to bed, upstairs

have: a drink, a meal, a party, a rest, a shower

make: a mess, a noise, a phone call, friends, the bed

take: an exam, a photo, the bus, the train, your coat off

Warm-up

1 Draw six columns on the board. Write one of these verbs at the top of each column: *do, get, go, have, make, take*. Ask students to copy this.
2 Give each student a copy of the Vocabulary grid.
3 Tell students that each vocabulary item goes with one of the six verbs. Elicit two examples and write them in the correct columns on the board.
4 Ask students to complete their table, either individually or in pairs.
5 Check the answers with the whole class. Students may suggest other possible answers that are not given in the Key vocabulary or used later in the game, e.g. *take a shower, make a meal*.

Main activity

1 Divide the students into groups of three or four. Give each group a copy of the board, a dice, and a set of counters.
2 Playing the game:
   ‣ Students take turns to throw the dice and move their counter along the squares.
   ‣ When they land on a square, they make a sentence about a student in the group using the picture and the word in the square, e.g. *Marco, I think you go swimming*.
   ‣ The other students have to decide whether the sentence is grammatically right or wrong. If the sentence is right, they stay where they are. If it is wrong, they go back two squares.
   ‣ If a student arrives on a square with a ladder, they may go up the ladder if they make a grammatically correct sentence. If they arrive on a square with a snake's head, they go down the snake.
   ‣ The winner is the first student to reach square 30.

Variation

The board can be used to practise particular grammatical structures at different levels, e.g.
present continuous   *He's going swimming. They're having a party.*
present perfect questions   *Have you been swimming today? Have you done the cleaning yet?*
conditional sentences   *If you don't take the bus, you'll be late for the party. If she goes dancing tonight, she'll be tired tomorrow.*

Follow-up

Show the class a picture of a man or woman. As a class the students build up a story about the person's daily routine, using language from the game, e.g.
Student A: *Every day Sally gets up at 7 o'clock and she has a shower.*
Student B: *Every day Sally gets up at 7 o'clock and she has a shower. She makes the bed, then …*
Continue in this way until all the students have had a turn.

Homework

A Write six questions using the vocabulary from the activity, then interview another person and write about them.
B Write six sentences about a day when you were very busy, using vocabulary from the activity.

Acknowledgement
We first came across the idea of using Snakes and Ladders in the language classroom in *Grammar Games* by Mario Rinvolucri (Cambridge University Press 1984).

Vocabulary grid

tired	your homework	swimming	the bed	a party	the cleaning
to bed	your coat off	the washing-up	a shower	upstairs	clubbing
a drink	a rest	angry	cold	the train	a noise
a phone call	running	the cooking	friends	the ironing	shopping
a meal	the bus	a mess	a photo	dressed	an exam

1.2

How special am I?

Level

Intermediate

Time

40–45 minutes

Aim

To practise vocabulary for talking about yourself and finding out what you have in common with other people

Materials

One copy of the sheet for each student in the class

Two dice for each group of four to six students

Key vocabulary

Positive characteristics
e.g. *energetic, fun-loving, generous, intelligent*

Negative characteristics
e.g. *bad-tempered, selfish, unreliable, untidy*

Hobbies and talents
e.g. *gymnastics, learning languages, photography, singing*

Places to go on holiday
e.g. *a city, an island, the beach, the mountains*

Significant years
e.g. *the year you first fell in love, the year you were born*

Influential people
e.g. *a friend, a neighbour, a teacher, a TV personality*

Treasured possessions
e.g. *a letter, a photograph, a piece of jewellery, a toy*

Favourite colours

Seasons of the year

Warm-up

1 Write these categories on the board: *Positive characteristics, Negative characteristics, Hobbies and talents, Places to go on holiday, Significant years, Influential people, Treasured possessions, Favourite colours, Seasons of the year.*
2 Ask students to suggest words and ideas that fit each category. Write two or three examples for each category on the board.

Main activity

1 Give each student a copy of the sheet and ask them to complete it individually. Set a time limit for this activity and monitor as necessary.
2 Check a few answers with the class. During feedback make sure that students understand the expression 'have something in common with someone', by asking them questions such as *Does anyone have something in common with Thomas?*
3 Divide the students into groups of four to six students. Give two dice to each group.
4 Tell students that they each start with ten points and their aim is to prove that they are different from the other students in the group. Students take turns to throw the dice and speak. For example, if a student throws a three and a five, they must speak about *either* item three *or* item five *or* item eight (the sum of the dice) from the sheet.
5 Explain that when they talk about their item they can be challenged by another student in the group, if that person can claim their own item has something in common with them, e.g. *My favourite season of the year is spring.* Then another student in the group might challenge that student by saying *My favourite season of the year is also spring.* If a claim is successful, the student who was challenged has to give away one point to the other student. Only one challenge may be made on each turn.
6 You may want to write the key points of the rules and scoring system on the board to help students.
7 The winner is the person with the most points at the end of the game.

Variation

Students take it in turns to play, but instead of throwing the dice, the person to the right of the player may say which item from the sheet they would like the player to talk about.

Follow-up

Ask students to write their name on the top of their sheet. Collect the sheets and redistribute them to the class. Ask a student to read out four different pieces of information about the person they have, without saying who they are describing. The other students have to guess who the person is.

Homework

A Write 100 words comparing yourself with one of the other people from your group. What do you have in common and how do you differ?
B Ask someone outside your class what their answers to the sheet would be (in your own language, if necessary) and then write a short profile of the person.

1   Three adjectives that describe me (positive or negative)

   ....

2   My favourite season of the year

   ....

3   Something I am very good at

   ....

4   Something I have done which I am proud of

   ....

5   Something I would like to be famous for

   ....

6   Something I would do if I had enough money

   ....

7   A year when something significant happened to me

   ....

8   A person who has influenced me a lot

   ....

9   A place where I would like to spend a holiday

   ....

10   A colour that makes me feel good

   ....

11   My ideal dinner guest or guests

   ....

12   My most treasured possession

   ....

1.3

The dating game

Level

Upper-intermediate
to advanced

Time

40–45 minutes

Aim

To practise expressing personal
likes, dislikes and preferences
in the context of choosing a
partner for a date

Materials

For Warm-up and Main activity,
one copy of the sheet for each
student

Sticky labels for the contestants

Six prize envelopes each
containing a slip of paper with
exotic holidays (e.g. a holiday
diving off the Great Barrier
Reef)

Key vocabulary

admire
be amazed
be committed to
be upset by
can't stand
disapprove of
feel at ease with
have a tendency to
keep your distance from

Warm-up

1 Elicit the meaning of the expression *can't stand*. Write an example sentence on the board: *I can't stand people who are selfish with their possessions.*

2 Give each student a copy of the sheet.

3 Check that students understand the other sentence beginnings. Tell them to choose five from the list and complete the sentences in any way they wish. Monitor as necessary.

Main activity

1 Explain that students are going to play a dating game in which the main contestant asks three other contestants personal questions in order to find a date. The audience then votes on which of the three contestants would be the best date for the main contestant.
   Note: If it is inappropriate or not possible to make this a real dating scenario with people of the opposite sex, you can say instead that students are looking for a suitable person to go on holiday with, or to share a house with, or to go into business with, etc.

2 Demonstrate how to add a question to the example sentence on the board, e.g.
   I can't stand people who are selfish with their possessions. What is your most precious possession and how could I persuade you to lend it to me?
   I have a tendency to forget people's birthdays. When is your birthday and how would you help me remember it?

3 Tell students to choose three of the five sentences they have written and add a question to each one. Monitor and help students as necessary.

4 Playing the game:
   ‣ Arrange four chairs at the front of the classroom, one for Student A (the person seeking a date) and three for Students B, C and D (the possible partners). The rest of the class will be the audience.
   ‣ Choose your set of contestants and give them a sticky label, on which they write an invented name. They should decide how old they are, what sort of job they do, and, for Student A, what their hobbies are and what sort of partner they are looking for.
   ‣ The host (this should be the teacher the first time the game is played) introduces the show and asks the contestants to introduce themselves.
   ‣ Student A reads out their first question and asks Students B, C and D to answer in turn. Repeat the process for the other two questions.
   ‣ After all the contestants have replied, the host asks members of the audience to summarise each contestant's answers. Then the audience votes to decide which of the three contestants wins the date.
   ‣ The two contestants who have not been chosen return to their seats. The winning pair choose a prize envelope and read out what they have won.

Variations

● Members of the audience take it in turns to decide what a suitable prize might be for each pair.
● Students play themselves instead of inventing a character to play in the game.

Follow-up

The game can be repeated with different contestants as often as time allows. After the game has been played once, you can ask a student to take on the role of the host.

Homework

A Complete the other five sentences from the sheet and give reasons for your answers.
B Write a personal advertisement describing yourself and saying why you are the perfect partner for the man or woman of your dreams.

1 **I really can't stand** ...

2 **I usually keep my distance from** ...

3 **I have a tendency to** ...

4 **I'm very committed to** ...

5 **I'm easily upset by** ...

6 **I strongly disapprove of** ...

7 **It always amazes me that** ...

8 **I really admire people who** ...

9 **I feel most at ease with people who** ...

10 **I feel least at ease with people who** ...

2.1

Family tree

Level

Elementary

Time

40–45 minutes

Aim

To practise the vocabulary of family relationships

Materials

For Warm-up and Main activity, one copy of the sheet for each student

For Variation, one copy of the sheet for each student

Key vocabulary

aunt
brother
brother-in-law
cousin
daughter
father
father-in-law
grandfather
grandmother
husband
mother
mother-in-law
nephew
niece
sister
sister-in-law
son
uncle
wife

Warm-up

1 Check that students understand the concept of a family tree. Then give each student a copy of the sheet and tell them that the diamonds are male relatives and the ovals are female relatives.
2 Tell students to look at the list of relatives. Tell them to find some of the relatives on the family tree by asking them some questions, e.g. *Where is Steve's aunt?*
3 Tell students to write the words in the correct spaces on the tree, leaving enough room to write a second word in each space later. Monitor as necessary and then check answers with the class. Finally, ask students what relation Steve is to his wife, i.e. husband.

Main activity

1 Divide the board into two columns with the headings *English male names* and *English female names*. Elicit nine male names and nine female names, and write them on the board.
2 Divide the students into pairs.
3 Tell Student A to write a man's name from the board in each diamond space on their copy of the family tree. Tell Student B to write a woman's name from the board in each oval space on their tree. They should not look at each other's tree.
4 Practise the question forms: *What's the name of ...? What is ... called?*
5 Students take turns to ask each other questions. Student A asks Student B about the women in Steve's family, e.g. *What's the name of Steve's mother? What's Steve's niece called?* and Student B asks Student A about the men in Steve's family. Students write the replies in the correct spaces on their tree.
6 When students have finished, they compare their trees to check their answers.

Variation

To make the game longer, each student can write in all the names from the board on their family tree so that they have to ask each other about every relative. For this variation students will need a second copy of the tree to write their answers on.

Follow-up

In pairs students use their completed family trees to practise making sentences about the relationships between other members of Steve's family, e.g. *Margaret is Jeff's mother-in-law.*

Homework

A Draw your own family tree. Choose six people from it and write a sentence about each one.
B If you have access to the Internet, use it to find out about a famous family. Write six sentences about them.

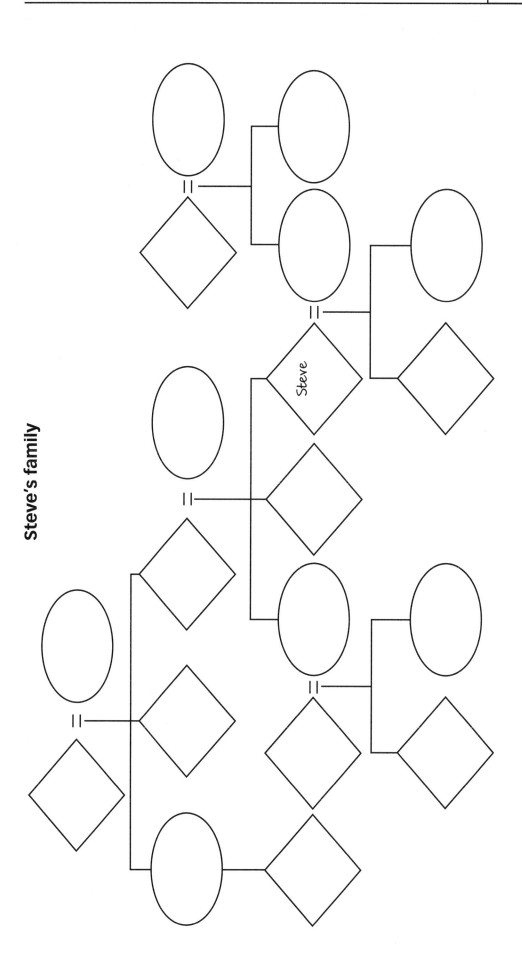

Steve's family

father	brother	sister	mother-in-law	nephew	aunt
mother	grandfather	brother-in-law	sister-in-law	niece	cousin
wife	grandmother	father-in-law	daughter	son	uncle

2.2

The happy couple

Note: Marriage break-up may not be an acceptable topic in some countries. The pictures on the photocopiable sheet are intended to allow for a variety of stories to emerge, and teachers may also choose to exclude certain pictures and vocabulary items if they seem inappropriate.

Warm-up

1 Select from the Key vocabulary the items you want to use and write them on the board in random order. Ask students to guess what the topic is.

2 Divide the students into pairs and ask them to organise the vocabulary in order of what happens first, second, third, etc. in a relationship.

3 Check students' answers and encourage discussion about possible orders. You may find that students do not all agree about the order depending on their culture and upbringing.

Possible order: *fancy, go on a date, go steady, fall in love, propose, get engaged, get married, go on honeymoon, move in together, settle down, start a family, grow tired of each other, separate.*

Main activity

1 Divide the students into pairs. If possible each pair should have one male and one female student, but the activity can still work with other pairings. Give each pair a set of pictures and questions.

2 Tell students to order the pictures to make a story about a marriage. They should give the characters in the pictures names and decide how old they are, what kind of work they do and how they spend their free time. Students should use the questions as prompts.

3 When students have decided on their story, they write notes based on the questions.

4 Join each pair with another pair to make groups of four. Explain to students that they should now each take on the role of one of the characters in their stories. Each pair is then interviewed by the other pair about their marriage. After the interviews, pairs decide on the future of the marriage, whether it is likely to be happy, etc.

Variation

Bring in magazine pictures of two men and two women that all the class will be able to see. Ask the students to choose one of the men and one of the women to be the couple in their story and tell them to give each character a name, a job, etc.

Follow-up

Go round the class to check how many of the imaginary marriages have been successful or not, and why. Ask students to nominate the best stories they have heard during the activity.

Homework

A Write the story you invented from the point of view of either the husband or wife, making sure that you include at least eight of the key vocabulary expressions dealt with in class.

B Write your own story, using past or future forms, imagining your ideal boyfriend/girlfriend or husband/wife. Begin with how they met or will meet, what they first said or will say to one another, etc.

Acknowledgement
This activity was inspired by a picture story in *Language in Use Pre-intermediate* by Adrian Doff and Christopher Jones (Cambridge University Press 1991).

Questions

Where did they meet?

What did they like about each other?

What was the first thing they said to each other?

Where did they go on their first date?

How often did they meet after that?

How soon did they fall in love?

What did their parents think about the relationship?

When did they decide to settle down?

How did he propose to her?

How long were they engaged before the wedding?

What was the wedding ceremony like?

Where did they go for their honeymoon?

How did their lives change after they got married?

2.3

Family idioms

Level

Upper-intermediate
to advanced

Time

35–45 minutes

Aim

To develop recognition of
idioms which relate to family
life and relationships

Materials

For Warm-up and Main activity,
one set of cards, cut up, for
each pair of students

One set of rules for each group
of four students

Key vocabulary

be as alike as two peas in a pod
*be as different as chalk and
cheese*
be the apple of your father's eye
be the black sheep of the family
*be tied to your mother's apron
strings*
be your mother's daughter
blood is thicker than water
follow in your father's footsteps
*twist someone round your little
finger*
*while the cat's away the mice
will play*

Warm-up

1 Divide the students into pairs and give each pair a set of cards.
2 Write on the board the first part of one of the idioms. Ask students to find the other half of that idiom and try to elicit the meaning.
3 Ask pairs to match the remaining halves. Then check answers with the whole class and discuss what each idiom means and how it can be used.

Main activity

1 Put each pair of students with another pair to make a group of four. Students combine their sets of cards.
2 Give each group a set of rules. Talk through the rules with the class and check that they understand them.
3 Let students play the game for an appropriate time. If a group finishes quickly, tell them to shuffle the cards and play the game again. Monitor and help as necessary.

Variation

Divide students into groups of four and give each group a set of cards. Students spread the cards face down on the table. Students then take it in turns to turn over two cards, making sure the rest of the group can see them. If the student thinks the cards make a pair, they can keep them, if not, they turn the cards face down again. The winner is the person who has collected the most correct pairs when all the cards have been taken.

Follow-up

Students stay in their groups and talk about people or situations in their own family that could be described using these idioms.

Homework

A Choose one of the idioms as the title for a story. Prepare to tell your story to the class. Your classmates will try to guess which idiom you chose as your title.
B Write sentences using each of the idioms from the activity.

be as alike as	two peas in a pod	be your mother's	daughter
be as different as	chalk and cheese	blood is	thicker than water
be the apple of	your father's eye	follow in	your father's footsteps
be the black sheep	of the family	twist someone round	your little finger
be tied to	your mother's apron strings	while the cat's away	the mice will play

Rules of the game – Family idioms

1 Shuffle the cards and place them face down on the table in a pile.

2 Take six cards each. Don't show them to the other players.

3 Spread the remaining cards face down on the table.

4 Take turns to play. The aim of the game is to arrange the cards in your hand to make three complete idioms. Turn over one of the cards on the table, trying not to let the other players see it. You can *either* pick this card up and keep it, if you think it completes an idiom, *or* turn it face down again on the table. If you decide to keep the card, you must put one of your other cards face down on the table. You must only have six cards in your hand at any time.

5 The first person to have three complete idioms is the winner.

3.1

What people do

Level

Elementary

Time

35–45 minutes

Aim

To practise words for everyday activities

Materials

For Warm-up, one copy of the sheet, cut up and put in an envelope, for each group of four students

One copy of the sheet, cut up and put in an envelope, for each student

For Homework, one copy of the sheet, not cut up

Key vocabulary

brush your hair
clean your teeth
cook
do your homework
drive a car
go shopping
listen to a CD
make tea
play football
post a letter
put on shoes
read a newspaper
ride a bike
run
sleep
swim
talk on the phone
wash your hair
watch TV
write a letter

Warm-up

1   Divide students into groups of four. Give each group an envelope of cards. Tell one student in the group to take all the pictures of a boy, one those of a girl, another those of a woman and the last student those of a man. Each student should have five cards.

2   Ask each student to write down what their person is doing in each picture, e.g. *The boy is cleaning his teeth.* Monitor and help as necessary.

3   When groups have finished, each student takes it in turn to tell their group what their person is doing. The other students write down any new verbs. Check any difficult vocabulary with the whole class. Collect the envelopes of cards.

Main activity

1   Divide students into pairs. Ask them to sit back to back with a table or flat surface in front of each of them. Give each student an envelope of cards.

2   Draw a three-by-three grid on the board and label the columns *A*, *B*, *C* and the rows *1*, *2*, *3*. Student A takes nine pictures out of the envelope and arranges them in three rows of three, like the grid on the board. Student B must not be able to see Student A's pictures.

3   Student B then asks Student A for information, e.g. *What is C1 doing?* Student A looks at what card they have in that position and replies, e.g. *The boy is cleaning his teeth.* Student B then takes that card from their envelope and places it in front of them in the correct position.

4   The game continues until Student B has arranged the nine pictures. Student A checks their partner's answers. Then Student B arranges nine pictures in a different order for Student A to work out.

Variation

If your class is already familiar with prepositions of place, students may play the same game in pairs, but without using a grid. Check students are familiar with *next to*, *above*, *below*, *between*, *to the left/right of*. The student who has arranged the nine cards then describes the arrangement to their partner, e.g. *The boy cleaning his teeth is next to the girl listening to a CD.* Their partner may ask questions to check the arrangement, e.g. *Is the boy who is cleaning his teeth to the left of the girl who is … ?*

Follow-up

1   Divide students into different pairs and make sure that each pair has an envelope of cards. Student A takes nine cards from the envelope and arranges them in three rows of three, like the grid on the board. Student B should not watch while Student A does this.

2   When Student A is ready, Student B looks at the pictures for half a minute. Student B then turns away and describes which pictures are in which positions, e.g. *C3 – The man is running.*

3   Student A gives Student B one point for each correct verb remembered and another point for being able to say correctly what position the card is in. Student B then selects and places cards for Student A to remember.

Homework

A   Write down the verbs describing the pictures on the sheet under one of these headings, e.g.

Things I do every day	Things I sometimes do	Things I never do
clean my teeth	*read a newspaper*	*play football*

B   Write 50 – 100 words about what you did yesterday, using as many as possible of the verbs illustrated on the sheet.

Acknowledgement
The idea for this activity was inspired by a seminar given at IATEFL 2001 by Anthea Home, EFL Games (www.eflgames.com), Switzerland.

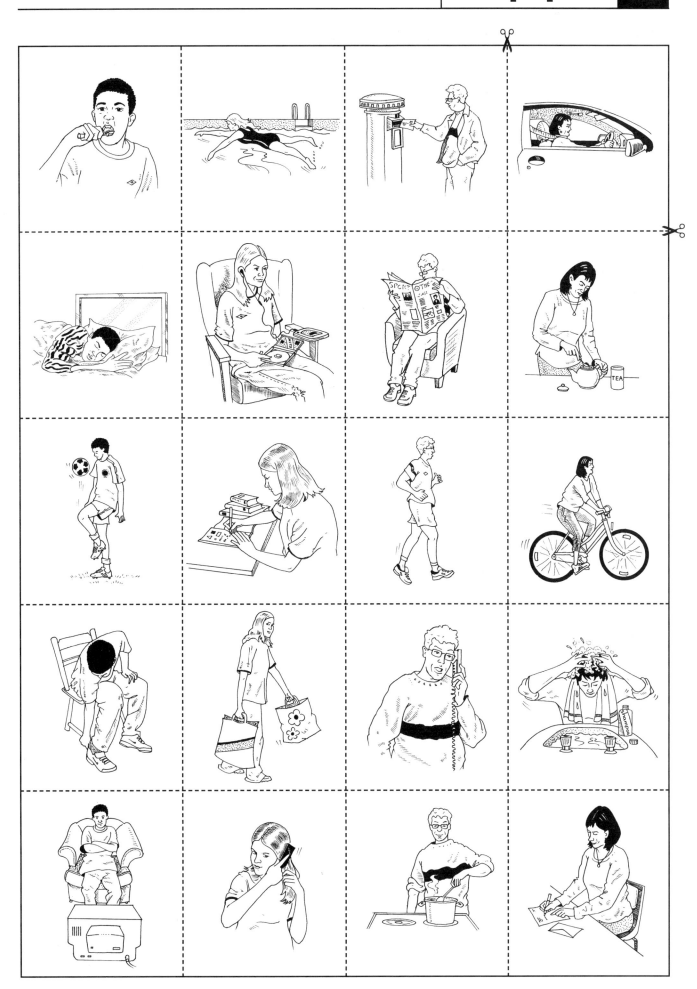

3.2

Change places if ...

Level

Intermediate

Time

25–35 minutes

Aim

To practise the language needed to talk about everyday activities

Materials

For Warm-up and Main activity, one copy of the sheet for each student

Key vocabulary

The key vocabulary for this activity may vary but is likely to be that covered in the possible answers below.

(1) had cornflakes / ate fruit / had coffee / didn't eat anything
(2) got up / had a shower
(3) bus/bike/car
(4) cleaned my teeth / got dressed
(5) did my homework / stayed at home
(6) petrol / some chocolate / a newspaper
(7) phoned / went out with
(8) letter / pen / book / cheque book
(9) the cinema / a friend's house / do some sport
(10) go to the cinema / do some sport / go out with friends
(11) several / no / two
(12) wrote / received
(13) the USA / Africa / Japan
(14) go shopping / have a lie-in
(15) bought food in
(16) have a party / do some gardening
(17) have a bath / read
(18) tennis / football / cards
(19) the newspaper / a magazine
(20) the radio / classical music

Warm-up

1 Give each student a copy of the sheet and brainstorm answers for two or three sentences with your class.
2 Then ask students to complete the sheet individually with things which are true for them. Monitor and help as necessary. Remind students that they can write negative as well as positive sentences, e.g. *I didn't write an email this morning*. Possible answers are suggested in the Key vocabulary section, but you or your students may well have many other interesting ways of completing the statements.

Main activity

You need a large clear area with no tables for this activity. If this is not possible, use the Variation. With very large classes, you may prefer to split the students into two or three groups.

1 Ask students to sit in a circle with their completed sheets. There should be one chair in the circle less than the number of students. The remaining student stands in the centre.
2 Demonstrate the game by reading out a sentence, e.g. *Change places with someone if you ate cornflakes for breakfast today*. While all those students who ate cornflakes for breakfast are changing places, the student in the middle tries to find a seat in the circle. The student who is left without a seat in the circle then stands in the middle and reads one of their sentences. Write up the prompt *Change places if you …* on the board and remind students to change their sentence from 'I' to 'you'.
3 Allow the game to continue until all or most students have had a turn standing in the middle.

Variation

If it is not possible or appropriate to play such an active game with your students, a game can be played using the same sheet but with all the students sitting down. Stress that this game depends on players being totally honest. Students take turns to choose a statement from the sheet and complete it in any way they wish. However, they should begin their statements: *Give yourself a point if you …*. After every student has had the chance to make two statements, all players total up their points to see who is the winner.

Follow-up

Ask students which were the most common activities and which were the most unusual activities.

Homework

A Write a diary entry in English about all the things you did yesterday.
B Write a letter to a pen friend describing a typical day in your life.

Acknowledgement
We learnt this activity from Paul Davis and Katie Plumb.

1 I .... for breakfast today.

2 I .... before I had breakfast this morning.

3 I came here by ....

4 I .... before I left home this morning.

5 I .... last night.

6 I bought .... yesterday.

7 I .... a friend yesterday evening.

8 I have a .... in my bag.

9 I am going to .... this evening.

10 I .... at least once a week.

11 I made .... phone call(s) last night.

12 I .... an email this morning.

13 I had a holiday in .... last year.

14 I .... most Saturdays.

15 I .... the supermarket last week.

16 I am going to .... at the weekend.

17 I usually .... before I go to sleep.

18 I played .... yesterday.

19 I read .... yesterday.

20 I usually listen to .... in the bath/car.

3.3

Check in cheerfully

Level

Upper-intermediate
to advanced

Time

35–45 minutes

Aim

To practise common phrasal
verbs and adverbs of manner

Materials

For Warm-up, one copy of the
sheet for each student

One copy of the sheet, cut up,
for each team of four to six
students. Put the Adverb cards
in one envelope and the
Phrasal verb cards in another
envelope.

Key vocabulary

See photocopiable sheet
opposite

Warm-up

1 Give each student a copy of the sheet. Ask students to tell you when they last did each of the phrasal verbs on the sheet, e.g. *I last checked in at the airport in August when I was on my way to Madrid.*

2 Discuss different verb phrases that would seem likely to go with the adverbs on the sheet, e.g. *to wait nervously for an exam result, to walk nervously into the dentist's surgery.* Check that students understand all the adverbs.

3 Collect in the sheets before beginning the Main activity.

Main activity

1 Divide the students into teams of four to six people. Give each team two envelopes: one containing the Adverb cards and one containing the Phrasal verb cards.

2 One student from each team picks one phrasal verb and one adverb from the envelopes. Tell students not to return the cards to the envelopes after use. This student then acts out the phrasal verb in the manner of the adverb for their team to guess what cards they picked. Students should use mime, not words. The other students may refer to their sheets if necessary.

3 When the team has guessed both the phrasal verb and the adverb correctly, the next student takes a card from each envelope and acts them out.

4 The game continues in this way until one team has acted and guessed all the phrasal verbs and adverbs from their envelopes.

Variation

This activity can be made more challenging by making adverb cards with less frequent adverbs or any adverbs you have been dealing with recently. You may also increase the challenge by introducing some different phrasal verb expressions for students to act out.

Follow-up

Divide students into pairs and ask them to write down which adverbs, from the sheet or other adverbs they know, would be most likely to collocate with each of the phrasal verbs from the sheet.

Homework

A Divide the adverbs from the sheet into three groups: *positive associations, negative associations, can have positive or negative associations.*

B Choose eight of the phrasal verb expressions and write a sentence saying how you usually do each of these things. You may use an adverb from the sheet or a different one if you prefer, e.g. *I usually tidy up a room reluctantly.*

Adverbs

angrily	bravely	calmly	carefully
cheerfully	clumsily	defiantly	despairingly
disgustedly	enthusiastically	gracefully	impatiently
miserably	nervously	proudly	rapidly
reluctantly	romantically	sleepily	timidly

Phrasal verbs

check in at the airport	dish up a meal	fill in a form	get out of a car
hand round some sweets	hang up your coat	heat up some soup	lean back in your chair
look for your bag	look out of the window	look round the room	pick up a coin
put on a hat	put on some make-up	put out the rubbish	sort out your bag
tidy up a room	tie up your shoelaces	turn off your alarm clock	wrap up a parcel

4.1

At home

Level

Elementary

Time

30–35 minutes

Aim

To revise and practise common vocabulary items relating to houses

Materials

For Warm-up and Main activity, one copy of the sheet, cut up, for each team of five to six students. Put each set in an envelope labelled Team A, Team B, etc.

For the Follow-up and Homeworks A and B, one sheet, not cut up, for each student

Key vocabulary

armchair
basin
bath
bed
bookcase
carpet
CD player
chair
chest of drawers
computer
cooker
cup
cupboard
curtains
door
fridge
glass
kettle
knife
lamp
mirror
plate
remote control
saucepan
shelf
shower
sofa
spoon
table
toothbrush
towel
TV
wardrobe
washing machine
wastepaper basket

Warm-up

1 Divide students into teams of five to six students, Team A, Team B, etc., and give each team a labelled envelope with a set of cut-up picture cards.
2 Ask teams to spread the picture cards on the table in front of them.
3 Name the items shown on the cards and ask teams to hold up the correct pictures. Do this as rapidly as possible with all the pictures, repeating any that the students are not sure of.

Main activity

1 Students return their envelope of cards and you place these on a table in front of you.
2 Explain that the aim of the game is for students to mime objects from their envelope for the rest of their team to guess. If necessary, demonstrate this by miming an object for the class.
3 One student from each team goes to the table and picks a card from their team's envelope, looks at it and then places it face down on the table. If a student is unsure of the word, they can whisper it to you to check.
4 Students then return to their team and mime the item for their team to guess. The students who are miming are not allowed to use any words.
5 Each team gets a point when they guess a word correctly and should keep note of their score. When the team has guessed the word correctly, the next student in turn goes to pick a card to mime.
6 Stop the game after about 15 minutes, or when all the cards have been used. The winning team is the one which has gained most points.

Variation

For a quicker game, the teams pick cards from just one envelope and the game is finished when all the cards have been used.

Follow-up

1 Divide students into pairs and give each student a copy of the sheet, not cut up.
2 Ask pairs to write the words for each of the things next to the pictures. Monitor as necessary and then check answers with the whole class.
3 If there is time, ask students to discuss with their partner which things they have in their own home.

Homework

A Ask students to write down the items from the sheet under these two headings:
Things I use everyday and Things I could live without.
B Write 12 of the words from the sheet in a phrase with an appropriate verb or adjective, e.g. to sit in an armchair, a large basin. Try to use a different verb or adjective each time.

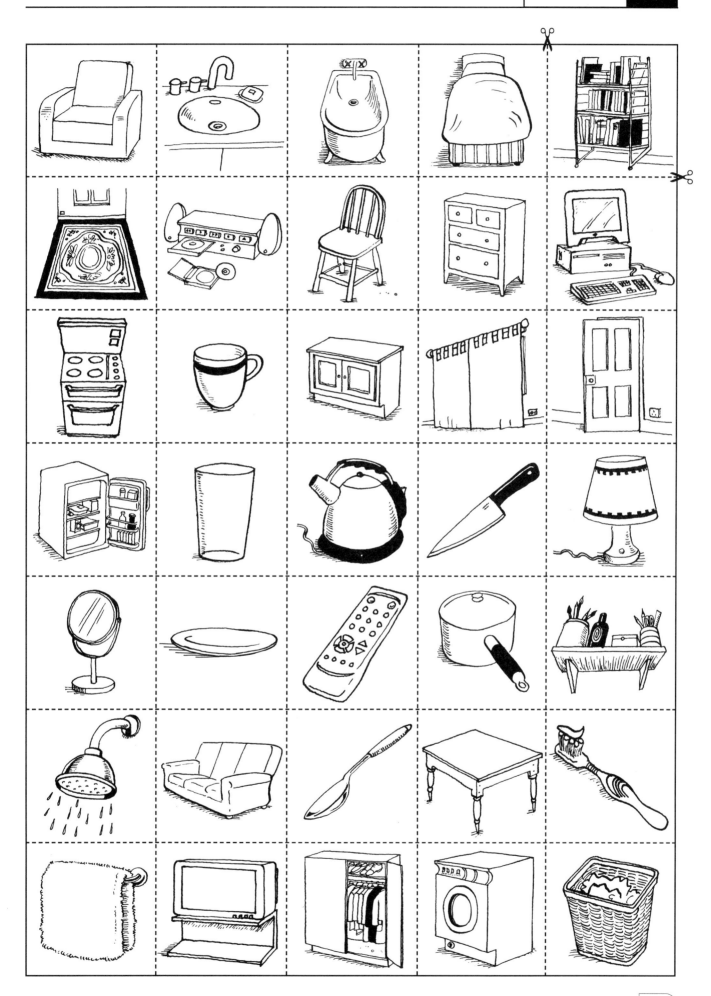

From *Games for Vocabulary Practice* by O'Dell & Head © Cambridge University Press 2003 **PHOTOCOPIABLE**

4.2

Fully furnished

Level

Intermediate

Time

40–45 minutes

Aim

To revise and practise vocabulary of furniture and household items

Materials

One copy of the sheet for each group of five students

One dice for each group of five students

For Follow-up, five extra copies of the sheet

Key vocabulary

Things likely to be found in specific rooms in a house/flat.

Kitchen
e.g. *frying pan, grater, rolling pin, sink, tin opener, washing machine*

Dining room
e.g. *bowls, crockery, cutlery, jug, table, table mats*

Sitting room
e.g. *armchair, bookcase, coffee table, rug, sofa*

Bedroom
e.g. *alarm clock, bedside table, chest of drawers, duvet, sheets, wardrobe*

Bathroom
e.g. *flannel, shower, soap dish, toilet, toothbrush, towel rail*

Warm-up

1 Ask students to close their eyes and imagine they are in their favourite room. What can they see around them?
2 Ask one or two students to describe their rooms in as much detail as possible. As they do this, elicit as much vocabulary relating to furniture and other household items as possible and try to cover all the main rooms of a house.

Main activity

1 Divide students into groups of five. If there are not enough students in your class for groups of this size, the activity can be done in smaller groups where students take responsibility for more than one room.
2 Give each group a copy of the sheet and a dice. Make sure that that each student also has a pen and paper.
3 Talk through the rules with students and check that they understand them. You may also want to demonstrate the game.
4 Discuss with the students what kind of items may be named, e.g. furniture (*table*, *chair*, etc.); household items (*knife*, *toothbrush*, etc.), but not food items or clothing. Explain that if there is any disagreement, the teacher's decision on what is appropriate is final.
5 Ask students to start the game. Stop the activity after 15 to 20 minutes.

Variation

The game can be made more challenging by introducing a memory element. When students throw the dice and get a room, they have to name all the items that have previously been used for that room and then have to add their own item.

Follow-up

1 Students work in groups according to the room they were responsible for, e.g. all the students who had the bathroom should form a group, etc.
2 In these new groups, students compare their lists and work out their individual scores as follows: they get one point for each item on their list and two additional points for any item that no other group thought of. Groups then calculate which of the original groups got the best 'bathroom' score, best 'kitchen' score, etc.

Homework

A Find a picture of a room from a magazine. Write a description of that room and comment on why you like or do not like it.
B Write 150 words describing your ideal flat and its contents.

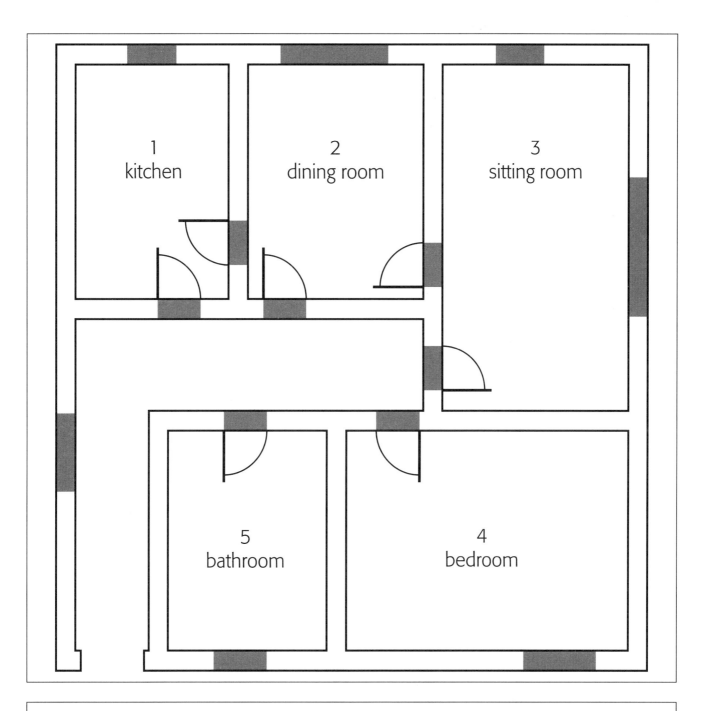

Rules of the game – Fully furnished

1 Take turns to throw the dice and then name something according to the number you throw. You have to name an item that you would find in a specific room according to the number on the dice you throw, so
   1 = kitchen 2 = dining room 3 sitting room 4 = bedroom 5 = bathroom

2 If you throw a 6, you can name another player and say which room that player must name an item for.

3 You may not name an item twice for the same room.

4 Each player in the group has responsibility for one, or more if necessary, of the five rooms. As things are named for that room, that player should make a note of them.

5 You miss a turn if you cannot think of a suitable item for the room required or if you repeat an item that has already been named for that room.

6 The winner is the person who missed the fewest turns.

4.3 Dream rooms

Level

Upper-intermediate
to advanced

Time

40–45 minutes

Aim

To practise talking about rooms,
their décor and furniture

Materials

For Warm-up, one copy of the
sheet for each student

One copy of the sheet for each
pair of students

Dictionaries may be useful

Key vocabulary

Adjectives to describe rooms
and their décor:
*air-conditioned, airy, antique,
beautiful, bright, comfortable,
cosy, elegant, functional,
luxurious, modern, original,
ornate, pastel shade, patterned
wallpaper, practical, quiet,
relaxing, shady, simple,
spacious, sunny, tidy, vibrant
colour, warm, white/off-white*

Things that might be found in
rooms:
*basketball net, computer with
Internet connection, fitted
carpet, full-length mirror, king-
size bed, latest games console,
lino, maps, oil paintings,
photos, polished wood,
postcards, posters, roomy
wardrobe, rug(s), state-of-the-
art music system, tiles, TV and
video, watercolours, well-lit
desk, well-stocked bookshelves*

Warm-up

1 Tell students that they have an unlimited budget to design and furnish their dream room. Ask them to close their eyes and think for about a minute what this room might be like.

2 Give each student a copy of the sheet and ask them to check the meanings of any new words in their dictionaries or by asking you.

3 Ask students to complete the sheet individually. Tell them not to put their names on their sheets.

Main activity

1 Explain that each student is going to ask questions to try to find someone with whom they have at least five things in common.

2 Give students some examples of questions they might ask each other, e.g. *Why is it important for you to have a cosy room? Whose photos would you have in your room?* Then ask students to move around the classroom with their sheets asking each other about the rooms they have designed.

3 When they have found someone with whom they have at least five things in common, they sit down with that person and discuss the rest of their answers.

4 Tell students to imagine that they will have to share their dream room with the person they have found. Give each pair a new copy of the sheet which they now have to complete as a pair. Ask them to decide what to do about the things that they did not originally have in common.

5 If students cannot find someone with whom they have five things in common, they must work with anyone and discuss how to complete their joint sheet.

6 Pairs present their shared dream room to the rest of the class.

Variation

If you have a large class, you may prefer to put students into groups of six to eight, instead of asking students to move around the classroom. In these groups they ask each other questions to find a partner who has the most similar room to them.

Follow-up

1 Collect the individually completed sheets. Make sure that students have not written their names on them.

2 Keep students in pairs and give each pair two sheets. Check that these do not include either of their own sheets. Tell students to try to identify whose sheets they have.

3 Each pair explains to the class whose sheets they think they have and why. After each pair has made their guess, the students who they think completed those sheets tell the class whether or not the guess was correct. At the end of the class, students whose sheets have not been identified should say which their sheets were.

Homework

A Write 150–200 words comparing your dream room to your actual room.

B Write 150–200 words about the most important things that you would want to have in your room, explaining why you would want them.

My dream room

Adjectives describing your ideal room

1 **Tick 2 adjectives from the list. Then write 2 other adjectives of your own.**

- [ ] airy
- [ ] spacious
- [ ] sunny
- [ ] cosy
- [ ] functional
- [ ] relaxing
- [ ] quiet

- [ ] tidy
- [ ] bright
- [ ] air-conditioned
- [ ] luxurious
- [ ] shady
- [ ] warm
- [ ] original

....

....

Things you'd have on your walls

2 **Tick two things for the walls and then write more about them, e.g. posters of football stars.**

- [ ] posters
- [ ] photos
- [ ] maps
- [ ] oil paintings
- [ ] watercolours
- [ ] mirrors
- [ ] postcards

....

....

The style and décor of your ideal room

3 **What kind of furniture would you prefer? Circle one in each pair.**

modern or antique

elegant or comfortable

beautiful or practical

simple or ornate

4 **What would you like on the floor? Tick a maximum of two.**

- [ ] fitted carpet
- [ ] polished wood
- [ ] tiles
- [ ] rug(s)
- [ ] linoleum

5 **What colour would you want for the walls? Tick one and then add more details.**

white or off-white

pastel shade

vibrant colour

patterned wallpaper

different colours for different walls

....

....

....

Furniture and objects in your ideal room

6 **Mark these items with either:**
A – would love this or
B – don't feel strongly about this or
C – don't want this
Then add two other things you'd like.

- [ ] state-of-the-art music system
- [ ] well-stocked bookshelves
- [ ] roomy wardrobe
- [ ] king-size bed
- [ ] full-length mirror
- [ ] basketball net
- [ ] well-lit desk
- [ ] TV and video
- [ ] computer with Internet connection
- [ ] latest games console

....

....

5.1

Finding places

Level

Elementary

Time

30–35 minutes

Aim

To practise saying where you can do different things in a town and explaining where places are using prepositional phrases

Materials

One copy of map A and one copy of map B for each pair of students

Key vocabulary

bank
car park
chemist
Chinese restaurant
cinema
clothes shop
football stadium
health centre
hotel
Internet café
library
newsagent
park
petrol station
post office
pub
sandwich shop
school
shoe shop
supermarket
swimming pool
train station
travel agency

between
next to
on the corner
on XXX Road
opposite

Warm-up

1   Ask students which places they go to in town and elicit the words from the Key vocabulary. Ask students to explain where a particular place is in their town, e.g. the cinema.
2   Draw a very simple street map with two or three places labelled and elicit prepositions of place from students, e.g. next to, between.

Main activity

1   Divide students into pairs, Student A and Student B, and ask students to sit facing each other.
2   Give Student A a copy of map A and give Student B a copy of map B. Tell students not to look at each other's maps. Explain that the maps are the same, but each student has information about places that their partner is looking for. Tell them that the places marked in bold are on both maps.
3   Tell students to look at the list of things that they need to do in town. Then students take turns to ask their partner *Where can I go to buy ...?* and their partner explains, e.g. *The sandwich bar is on Oak Avenue next to the pub, opposite the supermarket.* Students label the correct places on their maps.
4   When students have found all the places, tell them to compare their maps and check their answers.

Follow-up

1   In their pairs, students look at the maps together and take turns to say where places are.
2   After a few minutes one student turns their map over and their partner tests their memory by asking them where places are. Students win one point for each correct answer. After Student A has asked six questions, they turn over their map and Student B can ask Student A six questions.

Homework

A   Choose six facilities in your town and write sentences to describe their location using expressions of place.
B   Write a paragraph about some of the places you visited in a town recently and what you did there.

A

Where can I go to:

buy some shoes?

park my car?

eat a Chinese meal?

buy some medicine?

see a film?

watch a football match?

send a letter?

see a doctor?

buy a newspaper?

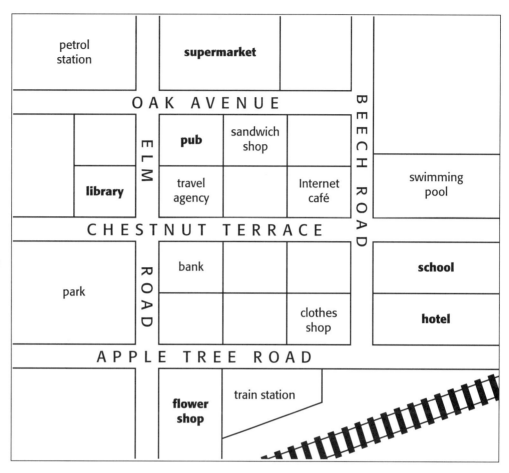

B

Where can I go to:

book a holiday?

buy a sandwich?

go swimming?

get travellers' cheques?

buy some clothes?

take my dog for a walk?

catch a train?

get some petrol?

check my emails?

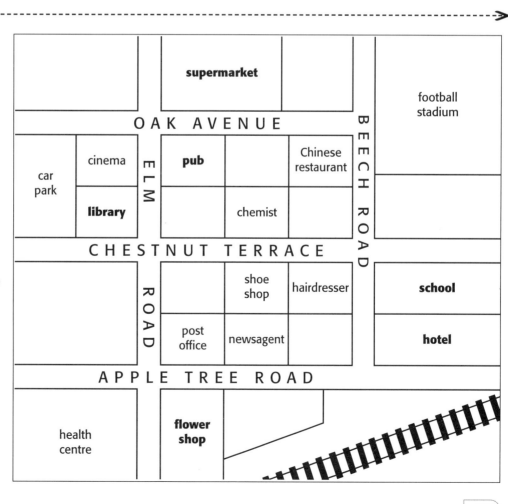

5.2

Mystery word pairs

Level

Intermediate

Time

35–45 minutes

Aim

To practise compound nouns which describe places and facilities in a town or city

Materials

For Warm-up and Main Activity, one set of cards, cut up, for each pair of students

For Homework A and B, one copy of the sheet, not cut up

Key vocabulary

art gallery
athletics track
business park
bus stop
car park
concert hall
department store
football stadium
health centre
industrial estate
law courts
parking meter
pedestrian crossing
phone box
police station
post office
rush hour
shopping mall
swimming pool
taxi rank
traffic lights
youth hostel

Note that although alternative pairings are possible, e.g. shopping centre, taxi meter, students will only be able to use all the cards if they make the pairings listed above

Warm-up

1 Give some examples of words which are formed by putting two other words together, e.g. *train ticket, table lamp, sports car.* Elicit more examples from the class.
2 Divide students into pairs and give each pair a set of cards. Ask them to find the word pairs for places in a town.
3 Check the answers with the whole class and explain any new vocabulary.

Main activity

1 Explain that students are going to make a story about an incident that happened in town yesterday, using all the word pairs they have made. Write the following sentence on the board: *Yesterday I was standing by the bus stop when I saw a strange man carrying a briefcase.*
2 Ask students to identify the word pair in the sentence, i.e. *bus stop*, and to put those word cards to one side.
3 Ask the class to provide the next sentence in the story. The sentence must contain another word pair. Write the sentence on the board, underline the word pair and tell students to put those cards to one side.
4 Students work in pairs and divide the remaining 20 word cards between them so that each student has 10 word pairs.
5 In their pairs, students take it in turns to add a new sentence to the story, beginning with the two sentences above. Students have to use one of their word pairs in the sentence and lay down the word pair on the table.
6 If a student is unable to make a sentence using one of their word pairs, they miss a go. Monitor and help as necessary. The first student to lay down all their cards is the winner.

Variation

This activity can be made more challenging by adding a memory element. When students lay down their cards and say their sentence, they first have to say the previous sentences in the correct order before they can say their new sentence. If they cannot remember all the sentences, they miss a turn.

Follow-up

Ask some pairs to tell their stories to the whole class. Then ask the class to vote on the best story they heard.

Homework

A Write down the story you made up in class and underline all the word pairs you used.
B Write down the word pairs in two lists: *My town has …* and *Places I wish my town had.*

bus	stop	pedestrian	crossing
rush	hour	youth	hostel
taxi	rank	traffic	lights
department	store	car	park
parking	meter	football	stadium
police	station	swimming	pool
phone	box	athletics	track
concert	hall	industrial	estate
art	gallery	business	park
health	centre	shopping	mall
law	courts	post	office

5.3

City life

Level

Upper-intermediate
to advanced

Time

35–40 minutes

Aim

To understand and use
vocabulary for describing some
common problems of city life

Materials

One set of 20 cards, cut up, for
each group of four students

Key vocabulary

See photocopiable sheet
opposite

Warm-up

1 Introduce the lesson with a brief discussion of where students live and what they like and dislike
   about the place where they live.
2 Ask them to list some of the problems of living or working in a big city. Write their ideas on the
   board. Introduce the words and expressions from the Key vocabulary, if they don't come up
   spontaneously, and check that students understand them.
3 Encourage students to briefly discuss the key issues relating to some of these problems.

Main activity

1 Divide students into groups of four and give each student in the group a set of five of the cards,
   including one blank.
2 Ask students to each complete their blank card with another common city life problem. Tell
   students in the same group to think of different problems from any of those their other group
   members have.
3 Explain that students are members of a committee which is responsible for deciding how the local
   council is to spend its annual budget. The groups have to compile a list of the top ten problems
   they would like to spend the budget on.
4 Tell students that they get a point each time they manage to persuade the other committee
   members that one of their five problem issues should be on the final list of ten.
5 After about 15 minutes ask students to write up their final list on the board and to count up their
   scores.

Variation

With smaller classes, divide students into pairs and give each student ten cards, including two blank
cards for them to fill in. Together students discuss the issues they feel are most important and
together they must create a list of the top ten issues.

Follow-up

Tell students to look at all the lists on the board. As a whole class they decide on a top ten list.

Homework

A Choose one of the problems discussed in class and write down some ideas for dealing with it.
B Write an essay of 150–200 words on the advantages and disadvantages of city life. Refer to at
   least eight of the issues you discussed in class.

deprived areas	disputes with neighbours	faulty burglar alarms	parking restrictions
litter in the street	vandalism	lack of public transport	graffiti
traffic gridlock	street beggars	potholes in street	night–time break-ins
late-night disturbances	schoolchildren playing truant	street lighting	industrial pollution

6.1

Name the country

Level

Elementary

Time

35–40 minutes

Aim

To practise the English names of countries

Materials

One copy of the sheet, cut up, for each group of four students

Key vocabulary

Arabic, Asia, Australia, Black Sea, Brazil, Denmark, East Asia, Europe, European, France, Greece, Italy, Japan, Mediterranean, Middle East, Portuguese, Russia, Saudi Arabia, South America, Switzerland, Turkey, United States

borders on, carnival, composer, island, kangaroo, mountain, Olympic Games, state, tunnel, volcano

Warm-up

1 Give the students two minutes to write down the names of as many countries as possible. Then divide students into pairs and ask them to compare their lists with each other.
2 Draw five columns on the board with the following headings: Europe, Asia, America, Australasia, Africa. Ask the students to call out the names of countries from their lists and tell you which column you should write them in.
3 Teach any items of Key vocabulary that you think your students will not know.

Main activity

1 Divide students into groups of four. Give one student in each group a copy of the crossword, one a copy of the A clues, one a copy of the B clues and one a copy of the C clues.
2 The student with the crossword chooses a missing word and tells the other students what number it is and how many letters are in it. The other students each read out their clues and then together students work out what the answer is and write it in the crossword.
3 If a group finishes quickly, ask them to think of another sentence for each of the countries in the crossword.
4 When all groups have finished, check answers with the whole class, paying particular attention to pronunciation.

Answers

(Across) 2 Greece 4 Japan 6 France 7 Russia 10 Brazil 12 Italy
(Down) 1 Denmark 3 Saudi Arabia 5 Turkey 8 United States 9 Switzerland 11 Australia

Variation

Divide students into three groups. Give one group the A clues, one the B clues and one the C clues. In these three groups students list all the countries they can think of which might be an answer to each clue. Then regroup the students so that there is one A, one B and one C student in each group. Together they work out what they think the answers will be before they see the crossword grid. Then give each group a copy of the crossword. Ask them to check their answers and complete the grid.

Follow-up

Divide students into pairs. Tell them to choose three different countries and write a clue for each of them. Then ask students to work with another pair and read out their clues for the other pair to guess the countries.

Homework

A List the names of all the countries from the crossword together with the name of their capital city and the main national language.
B Write six sentences about which of the countries in the crossword you would most like to visit and why.

A clues

Across

2   This Mediterranean country has lots of islands.
4   This country is in East Asia.
6   This country is famous for cheese and wine.
7   This country is very very big.
10 This country is in South America.
12 This country has a famous volcano called Mount Vesuvius.

Down

1   This country is famous for bacon and butter.
3   The language of this country is Arabic. (two words)
5   This big country is partly in Europe and partly in Asia.
8   This country is famous for jazz, hot dogs and jeans. (two words)
9   This country is in the middle of Europe.
11 This country is a very big island.

B clues

Across

2   This country had the first Olympic Games.
4   This country has four main islands.
6   There is a tunnel under the sea between this country and England.
7   This country has very cold winters.
10 This country has a famous carnival.
12 This European country is long and narrow.

Down

1   The capital city of this country begins with the letter C.
3   This country is in the Middle East. (two words)
5   This country borders on the Black Sea.
8   The language of this country is English. (two words)
9   This country is famous for chocolate and watches.
11 People speak English in this country.

C clues

Across

2   The capital city of this country begins with the letter A.
4   This country has a famous mountain called Mount Fuji.
6   This is one of the largest countries in Europe.
7   Some famous composers were born in this country.
10 The language of this country is Portuguese.
12 This country is famous for art and music.

Down

1   This country is in the north of Europe.
3   This country produces a lot of oil. (two words)
5   The capital city of this country begins with the letter A.
8   This country has many different states. (two words)
9   There are many high mountains in this country.
11 This country is the home of the kangaroo.

6.2

Happy holidays

Level

Intermediate

Time

30–40 minutes

Aim

To practise explaining what you want when you do not know the exact name for an item

Materials

For Warm-up, one set of Item cards, not cut up, for each pair of students

One set of Holiday cards, cut up, for each group of four students

One set of Item cards, cut up, for each group of four students

Key vocabulary

Suggested match between items and holidays:

A month on a desert island: *binoculars, book "Poisonous Plants", canoe and paddle, fishing rod, mosquito net, sun cream, torch*

Walking to the North Pole: *book "Wildlife of the Arctic", chocolate and tinned food, compass, first-aid kit, hat and gloves, skis, thermometer*

Cycling across the USA: *American English phrasebook, bicycle lights, bicycle pump, book "The USA from Coast to Coast", cycling shorts, massage oil, puncture repair kit*

Trekking in the Himalayas: *map of the Himalayas, plasters, rope, rucksack, sleeping bag, video camera, walking boots*

Warm-up

1 Elicit some examples of an adventure holiday, e.g. hang gliding, bungee jumping.

2 Ask if anyone in the class has ever been on an adventure holiday. Ask them where they went, what they did and what they took with them.

3 Divide students into pairs and give each pair a copy of the Item cards, not cut up. Elicit the vocabulary for the items and ask students what kind of holiday the items would be useful for.

Main activity

1 Divide the class into groups of four and explain that each member of the group is going on a different kind of adventure holiday.

2 Give each group a set of Holiday cards and a set of Item cards, and tell students not to look at them. Tell students to take one Holiday card each and to divide the Item cards equally between them. Tell students to now look at their cards but to keep them hidden from the rest of the group.

3 The aim is for each player to collect the seven items which they most need to pack for their particular holiday, without giving away the secret of what the holiday is. The items roughly correspond to seven per holiday. However the possibility that more than one person might want certain items makes the activity more interesting, as they then have to negotiate.

4 Playing the game:
   ‣ Students take turns to speak. They can address any other member of the group.
     Either the student can request a particular item from another person, e.g. *Do you have a bicycle pump?* If the person has that item, they give it to the student. In return the student gives them one of their items which they do not need.
     Or the student can offer another person an item which they do not want to keep, e.g. *I have a map of the Himalayas. Do you need it?* If the person needs that item they take it and give the student one of their items which they do not need in return.
   ‣ Students should always have seven items.
   ‣ If an offer or a request is successful, then the player may have another turn, up to a maximum of three turns in any one go.
   ‣ Students exchange items in this way until each person in the group has a set of seven items that they think will be useful for their holiday.
   ‣ Each person in turn names their seven items, and the other group members try to guess what sort of holiday it is.

Variation

Divide students into groups of four. Give each student seven item cards and one holiday card. Tell students that they have to justify to the others in the group why each of the items would be useful for their particular holiday. They get a point for each item that they can justify to the satisfaction of the rest of the group.

Follow-up

Divide students into groups of people with the same holiday card. Ask the groups to compare the items they chose. Were there any differences? Who had the best set of seven items? Ask students to list ten more things they would take on a holiday of this kind.

Homework

A List all the things that you usually like to take with you on holiday.

B Write a story of 100–150 words that begins or ends with the words *Thank goodness I had taken it on holiday with me!*

Holiday cards

1 A month on a desert island	**2** Walking to the North Pole
3 Cycling across the USA	**4** Trekking in the Himalayan mountains

Item cards

1 Phrasebook	2 bicycle lights	3 bicycle pump	4 binoculars
5 Poisonous Plants	6 Guide book	7 Wildlife of the Arctic	8 Canoe & paddle
9 chocolate & tinned food	10 Compass	11 bicycle shorts	12 First aid kit
13 Fishing rod	14 hat and gloves	15 Map	16 Massage oil
17 Mosquito net	18 PLASTERS	19 bicycle repair kit	20 rope
21 rucksack	22 skis	23 sleeping bag	24 Sun cream
25 Thermometer	26 Torch	27 video-camera	28 Walking boots

6.3

Colourful holiday collocations

Level

Upper-intermediate
to advanced

Time

40–45 minutes

Aim

To encourage students to create
their own colourful collocations
of the kind used in tourist
brochures to describe attractive
holiday destinations

Materials

One set of Adjective and Noun
cards, cut up, for each group of
three to four students

Dictionaries may be useful

For Homework B, a copy of the
sheet, not cut up, for each
student

Key vocabulary

Suggested collocations:

cobbled/hidden/winding **alleys**
abandoned/isolated/sandy
beaches
craggy/ precipitous/ towering
cliffs
dramatic/rocky/rugged
coastline
parched/rain-soaked/
undulating **countryside**
barren/parched/sun-drenched
deserts
dense/lush/verdant **forests**
dusky/windswept /wooded **hills**
dusky/remote/shimmering
horizons
grassy/leafy/lush **meadows**
breathtaking/dramatic/
spectacular **panoramas**
jagged/snow-capped/towering
peaks
barren/craggy/crumbling **rocks**
grassy/undulating/wooded
slopes
ice-cool/meandering/
shimmering **streams**
cobbled/tree-lined/winding
streets
hidden/picturesque/plunging
valleys
abundant/lush/overgrown
vegetation
breathtaking/dramatic/
spectacular **views**
ancient/crumbling/remote
villages

Warm-up

1 Dictate the list of features listed in bold in the Key vocabulary (i.e. *alleys, beaches, cliffs,* etc.). Tell the students to write these nouns in a list down one side of a piece of paper. Check that they understand each of the words.

2 Ask students to think of adjectives which are used, for example in holiday brochures, to describe these different features of the landscape, e.g. *stunning/spectacular beaches*. There is no need to elicit the exact vocabulary used in the activity because this will emerge during the activity.

3 Ask students which adjectives could collocate with which nouns, e.g. *spectacular cliffs/panoramas/coastline*, etc.

Main activity

1 Divide the students into groups of three to four.

2 Give each group a set of Adjective and Noun cards and ask them to find appropriate adjective-noun collocations. There is a range of possible collocations, so encourage students to see how many different collocations they can find, using dictionaries if necessary. There are at least three possible adjectives for each noun. Check some collocations with the class and write any difficult vocabulary on the board.

3 When students are familiar with all the vocabulary, ask them to sort the cards back into nouns and adjectives. Then ask students to turn the cards face down and spread them on the table, the nouns on one half, the adjectives on the other.

4 Students take turns to play. The first student turns over two cards – one adjective and one noun – and places them on the table so that the others can see. The student says whether they think the two words collocate successfully. If they say 'no', they put the cards back in the same places, face down. If they say 'yes' , the student has to produce a sentence using the collocation correctly. The rest of the group judges whether the sentence is acceptable, and if it is, the student keeps the two cards.

5 Students should try to remember where the cards are so that they can pick correct pairs. The students continue, until all the noun cards have been taken. Monitor and help as necessary.

6 The student with the most cards at the end is the winner.

Variation

For a quicker game, students play in groups of three to four and begin by selecting just one Adjective card to match each of the twenty Noun cards. They then play with those forty cards and put the unwanted cards aside. They place the forty cards face down on the table. Players take it in turns to turn over two cards. If they find a collocating pair, they keep the cards and have another turn. If they do not find a pair, they put back the two cards in the same places. The winner is the player with most cards at the end of the game.

Follow-up

Discuss with the class which of the possible collocations for each noun would be most appropriate for the area where they are.

Homework

A Write the text for a tourist brochure based either on a picture, or their memory of a place they know well.

B Choose ten adjectives from the lesson and find one new noun which collocates with each of them, e.g. *snow-capped mountains*.

Adjectives

windswept	barren	sun-drenched	meandering
breathtaking	jagged	dusky	rocky
snow-capped	winding	verdant	parched
rugged	precipitous	craggy	isolated
dense	spectacular	abundant	picturesque
cobbled	lush	plunging	dramatic
undulating	sandy	hidden	leafy
grassy	ice-cool	ancient	crumbling
towering	remote	overgrown	abandoned
wooded	rain-soaked	tree-lined	shimmering

Nouns

horizons	slopes	villages	vegetation
streams	cliffs	alleys	valleys
beaches	meadows	rocks	peaks
forests	countryside	deserts	views
panoramas	streets	coastline	hills

7.1

What I had for dinner last night

Level

Elementary

Time

30–35 minutes

Aim

To practise basic vocabulary of food and drink

Materials

For Warm-up, one copy of the sheet, not cut up, for each student

One copy of the sheet, cut up, for each group of four to eight students

Key vocabulary

apple
banana
bar of chocolate
biscuits
bowl of pasta
bowl of rice
cake
carrot
chicken
chips
cup of coffee
fish
garlic
glass of milk
glass of orange juice
grapes
hamburger
ice cream
lemon
loaf of bread
mushroom
onion
orange
pineapple
pizza
sausages
sweets
tomato

Warm-up

1   Ask students what they had for dinner last night. Elicit as many different items of food and drink as possible.
2   Give each student a copy of the sheet, not cut up, and ask them to write the names of the items beside each of the pictures. Ask students to write 'a(n)' or 'some' next to the name, e.g. an apple, some garlic, etc.
3   Check answers with the whole class.

Main activity

1   Divide students into groups of four to eight students. Give each group a set of picture cards, cut up, including the four blank cards.
2   Playing the game:
   ‣   The first student picks a card, e.g. lemon, and says *I had a lemon for dinner last night.* The student keeps that card.
   ‣   The next student picks a card, e.g. bowl of rice, and says *I had a lemon and a bowl of rice for dinner last night.* The student keeps that card.
   ‣   Each student has to list all the previous cards in the correct order before they say what is on their card. If they cannot remember a card, the student with that card shows it to them as a clue.
   ‣   If a student picks a blank card, they can choose their own food item.
   ‣   The game continues until all the cards have been picked.

Variation

For a more challenging game, each time it is their turn students name two food items – one that is pictured on the card and one that they choose themselves, e.g. *I had a lemon and a hot dog for dinner last night.* They can choose any item as long as it has not been mentioned by another student. If they choose a blank card, they only need to name one item.

Follow-up

1   Divide students into pairs and ask them to discuss what they would most like to eat that evening using some of the food illustrated on the sheet from the Warm-up, or mentioned during the game.
2   Pairs compare their thoughts about what they would like to eat that evening with the rest of the class.

Homework

A   Write a grid of menus for a three-course meal for each day of the week. Choose different food for each day of the week, using items from the sheet and your own ideas, e.g.

Day	First course	Second course	Third course
Sunday	Tomato soup	Fish with rice	Pineapple

B   Write down all the words for the food and drink items from the sheet in one of three groups: *I love*; *I like*; *I don't like*.

7.2

Twenty questions

Level

Intermediate

Time

40–45 minutes

Aim

To practise verbs and adjectives used with food items

Materials

For Warm-up, one copy of the sheet for each student

One set of picture cards, cut up, for each group of five to six students

Key vocabulary

Food preparation:
bake, barbecue, blend, boil, chop, cooked, dessert, dry, fattening, fry, grate, grill, healthy, pickle, poach, raw, roast, savoury, slice, squeeze, steam, stew, sticky, stir fry, sweet, toast

Foodstuffs:
apricot, beans, (bread) roll, cabbage, cheese, cream, cucumber, duck, egg, garlic, grapefruit, grapes, ice cream, lamb chop, lentils, mustard, nuts, olives, oysters, peas, pepper, potato, prawns, raisins, rice, salmon, salt, sardines, spring onion, steak, strawberry, sweetcorn, (sweet) pepper, vinegar, yogurt

Warm-up

1 Tell students you are thinking of a food item, e.g. a banana. Tell them to ask you yes/no questions to try to identify what the food item is, e.g. *Is it a vegetable? Can you fry it?*

2 Count how many questions the students ask until they guess the item. If they have not guessed after asking 20 questions, tell them the answer.

3 Give each student a copy of the sheet. Go through the questions with them and elicit or explain any of the words that they do not understand. Check they understand all the food items.

Main activity

1 Divide students into groups of five to six. Give each group one set of picture cards and tell them to place them face down in a pile on the table. Ask students to fold over the sheet from the Warm-up so that they can only see the questions.

2 Students take it in turns to pick a card. Their team must ask them yes/no questions, including questions from the sheet, to guess what was on the card.

3 The groups have to guess the picture by using no more than 20 yes/no questions.

4 The student with the card keeps a note of how many questions have been asked. If the group has not guessed the word by question 20, the student wins a point and shows the group the picture.

5 The game continues until each student has had at least two chances to pick a card. The student with the most points wins.

Variation

Instead of cutting up the pictures, allow students to choose any food item they want from the sheet. They should not choose an item which has already been used once.

Follow-up

In their groups of five to six, ask students to look at the sheet and plan a meal for their classmates using the food illustrated. They should try to use as many as possible of the words in the questions to describe how they would prepare the meal. Then each group presents their suggestion to the rest of the class and the class votes on the most appetising meal.

Homework

A Write a recipe using as many as possible of the words from the activity.

B Write down each of the verbs in questions 5 and 6 together with two things that could be used as objects for the verb, e.g. *You can grate cheese and carrots.*

Questions

1   Is it sweet / savoury / sticky / healthy / fattening?
2   Do you usually eat it raw / cooked?
3   Would you use it in a soup / salad / sandwich / cake / drink?
4   Would you eat it with meat / fish / a dessert?
5   Could you grate / chop / slice / blend / squeeze it?
6   Do you bake / barbecue / boil / roast / fry / grill / poach / stir fry / stew / steam / toast / dry / pickle it?

apricot	grapefruit	(bread) roll	cabbage	cheese
mustard	steak	cream	cucumber	egg
garlic	ice cream	lamb chop	sardines	lentils
nuts	olives	spring onion	oysters	peas
pepper	potato	prawns	raisins	rice
salmon	salt	duck	strawberry	sweetcorn
yoghurt	grapes	vinegar	(sweet) pepper	green beans

7.3

Odd one out

Level

Upper-intermediate
to advanced

Time

40–45 minutes

Aim

To practise language relating to
the theme of eating and
drinking and to practise
explaining differences between
items

Materials

For Warm-up and Main activity,
one copy of the sheet for each
pair of students

One copy of the Suggested
answers for each pair of
students

Dictionaries may be useful

Key vocabulary

See photocopiable sheet
opposite

Vocabulary used to define and
differentiate
e.g. *are types of, things used
for, the odd one out is*

Warm-up

1 Divide students into pairs. Give each pair a copy of the sheet.

2 Each picture illustrates one of the words from the sheet. Ask students to identify the pictures on the sheet.

3 Ask students to identify categories for the eight sets.

Main activity

1 Check that students understand the term 'odd one out'. Explain that it is possible to find a reason why each word in each set can be considered as the odd one out. Give an example from the Suggested answers below and elicit some more reasons from the class.

2 Ask each pair to look at two of the eight sets. Try to give the different pairs different sets.

3 Allow the pairs 10 minutes to find as many odd ones out as possible and to write down the different reasons. If a pair has finished their own sets, they may choose another set from the sheet.

4 Ask pairs to read out their answers to the whole class. Suggested answers are given below, but allow other logical suggestions. Give pairs one point for each correct or logical answer, and two points if a pair has found an odd one out for every word in a set.

5 Give each student a copy of the Suggested answers below and ask them to read the answers to the ones that they did not find. Discuss any questions that arise from this.

Variation

This game can be done as a whole class activity. Divide the class into two teams. Call out the words in the sets in turn. Give a mark to whichever team is first to explain why a particular word could be the odd one out.

Follow-up

In pairs students prepare a similar set of four food items for the rest of the class. The pairs must be prepared to explain why each of the four items in their set could be considered odd. Pairs write their sets on the board for discussion by the class.

Homework

A Write sentences illustrating how each of the verbs in sets 3 and 5 is used.

B Write the words in sets 2, 4 and 7 in appropriate phrases or collocations, e.g. *a mug of coffee*.

Suggested answers

1 Fruits – **orange**: skin not normally eaten; **tomato**: seeds normally eaten; **cherry**: you usually eat more than one; **plum**: comes in different colours

2 Crockery – **mug**: has a handle; **saucer**: you don't drink out of one; **bowl**: you use a spoon with; **tumbler**: usually made of glass, not pottery

3 Cooking verbs – **boil**: requires water; **fry**: requires oil or butter; **roast**: done in an oven; **grill**: heat applied directly to food

4 Kitchen utensils – **skewer**: remains in place during cooking; **grater**: used for preparing, not handling food; **tongs**: a plural noun; **spatula**: can be made of plastic or wood instead of metal

5 Eating verbs – **chew**: not about liquid; **sip**: does not focus on noticeable mouth movements; **swallow**: can be done with nothing in your mouth; **lap**: animals, not people, do this

6 Meat items – **mince**: does not include a bone; **chop**: can be grilled; **shoulder**: the only one that is not also used as a verb in cooking; **joint**: may or may not include a bone

7 Used for cleanliness – **table mat**: is usually hard; **napkin**: touches your lips; **tablecloth**: everyone at the table shares; **dishcloth**: not put on the table

8 Fruits and vegetables – **aubergine**: often eaten hot; **beetroot**: same colour inside as outside; **watermelon**: not red on outside; **radish**: you usually eat more than one

1 orange, tomato, cherry, plum

2 mug, saucer, bowl, tumbler

3 boil, fry, roast, grill

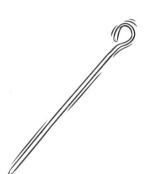

4 skewer, grater, tongs, spatula

5 chew, sip, swallow, lap

6 mince, chop, shoulder, joint

7 table mat, napkin, tablecloth, dishcloth

8 aubergine, beetroot, watermelon, radish

8.1

Who am I?

Level

Elementary

Time

30–40 minutes

Aim

To practise language of physical descriptions – hair, build and clothes

Materials

For Warm-up and Main activity, one copy of the sheet, cut up and put in an envelope, for each student

For Homework A, one copy of the sheet, not cut up

Key vocabulary

Hair:
bald, beard, moustache, curly/dark/fair/long/short/straight hair

Height:
medium height, short, tall

Size:
large, medium build, slim

Clothes:
boots, coat, dress, glasses, handbag, hat, jeans, sandals, shirt, shoes, shorts, skirt, suit, sunglasses, sweater, tie, top, trousers, t-shirt

Warm-up

1 Give each pair of students an envelope containing a set of picture cards and ask them to spread them out in front of them.

2 Choose a picture and pretend to be the person on the picture. Describe yourself in five sentences without mentioning your name. E.g. *I have fair hair, not dark hair. I am a woman. My hair is short, not long. I am wearing …,* etc.
After five sentences, ask students to guess who the person is.

3 Repeat step 2 two or three times. Then elicit any other words from the Key vocabulary that your students need to know.

Main activity

1 Give each student an envelope containing a set of picture cards. Students then play in their pairs. Student A puts all their pictures face up on the table.

2 Tell Student B to choose one picture from their own envelope and look at it without showing it to Student A. Student B pretends to be the person on the picture.

3 Student A must find out who Student B is. Student A asks yes/no questions,
e.g. *Are you female?*
If B says 'yes', then A can put all the male pictures to one side.
Have you got dark hair?
If B says 'no', then A can put all the pictures of women with dark hair to one side.

4 Play continues until Student A guesses Student B's name. Then it is Student A's turn to choose a card.

5 Allow the game to continue for 10–15 minutes or as long as you feel appropriate.

Follow-up

Ask a student to describe another student in the class without naming them, by giving information about their hair, their clothes, etc. The other students try to guess who is being described.

Homework

A Choose four pictures from the sheet. Imagine that the people in the pictures all know each other. Write a paragraph about them. Describe them and also invent more information about them. For example, *Emily and Anna are sisters. Anna is tall and slim with short curly hair. Dave is Anna's boyfriend. He is a student …*

B Write a description of the people in your family, using the vocabulary from the activity.

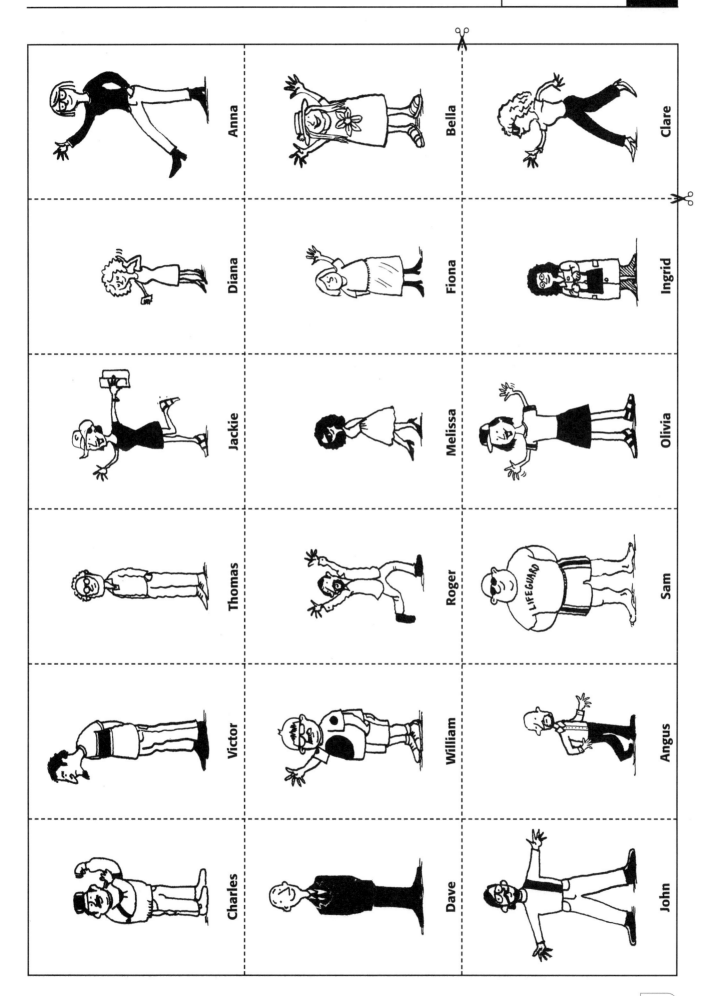

8.2

Compound adjective dominoes

Level

Intermediate

Time

40–45 minutes

Aim

To practise compound adjectives for describing people

Materials

One set of dominoes, cut up, for each group of four students

Dictionaries may be useful

Key vocabulary

First parts of compound adjectives:
big, blue, broad, brown, curly, dark, fair, hard, light, long, narrow, open, pig, round, short, single, straight

Second parts:
backed, eyed, faced, haired, handed, headed, hearted, minded, necked, shouldered, skinned

Compound adjectives formable from these parts include:
(Appearance) *big-eyed, blue-eyed, broad-shouldered, brown-eyed, brown-haired, brown-skinned, curly-haired, dark-eyed, dark-haired, dark-headed, dark-skinned, fair-haired, fair-headed, fair-skinned, light-haired, light-skinned, long-faced, long-haired, round-eyed, round-shouldered, short-haired, straight-backed, straight-haired*

(Character) *big-headed, big-hearted, broad-minded, fair-minded, hard-headed, hard-hearted, light-headed, light-hearted, narrow-minded, open-handed, open-hearted, open-minded, pig-headed, single-handed, single-minded*

Other combinations may also be possible

Warm-up

1 Divide the board into four columns. In the far left column write the first parts of the compounds as listed in the Key vocabulary, in the next column the second parts. At the top of the third and fourth columns write *Appearance* and *Character* respectively.

2 Ask students to suggest words by combining elements from the first two columns and ask students to tell you whether to write the words in the *Appearance* column or the *Character* column.

3 Elicit any other words from the Key vocabulary list and put them on the board under the appropriate heading.

Main activity

1 Divide students into groups of four. Give each group a set of dominoes.

2 Tell each student to take eight dominoes and place the rest in a pile face down on the table.

3 The first student places one of their dominoes face up on the centre of the table. The next student places one of their dominoes either before or after it to form a compound adjective. E.g. If the first student places the *backed/big* domino, the next student could place, for example, the *hearted/straight* domino to the left, forming the word *straight-backed*, or place the *hearted/straight* domino to the right, forming the word *big-hearted*.

4 If the next student cannot form a word from the dominoes in their hand, they must pick one from the pile, forming a word with it if possible. If it is impossible, the player keeps that domino and play passes to the next student.

5 The winner is the first student to use all of their dominoes. If there is time, students can shuffle the dominoes and play the game again.

6 When students have finished, ask groups to read their domino line to the class. The rest of the class decides whether they agree with all the compounds. Discuss any new or difficult vocabulary.

Variation

Students work in pairs with one set of dominoes. They produce as long a continuous line of dominoes as possible, so that compound nouns are formed as you pass from one domino to the next, e.g. *-backed/big-hearted/brown-eyed/curly*, etc. Students may place dominoes to the left or the right of the line. Stop after an appropriate time. The pair with the longest continuous line wins.

Follow-up

1 Divide the students into pairs and tell them to write down the names of all the students in the class.

2 Ask students to look at the two columns of compound adjectives under *Appearance* and *Character*, which you wrote on the board during the Warm-up. Ask students to write down one compound adjective to describe each student. They should not write the same adjective for more than one student.

3 Call the names of the students in turn and pairs tell you which adjectives they wrote for that student.

Homework

A Write down all the compound adjectives from this activity that could be used to describe your appearance and character.

B Write down ten compound adjectives from the activity that you particularly want to learn and find two collocating nouns for them, e.g. *a light-hearted remark, a light-hearted film*.

Acknowledgement

This idea was inspired by the word-building domino games devised by Paul Davis and Mario Rinvolucri.

-backed	big	-backed	light	-haired	big
-backed	dark	-headed	narrow	-handed	blue
-handed	broad	-hearted	brown	-eyed	curly
-haired	open	-haired	dark	-skinned	short
-eyed	light	-eyed	light	-faced	fair
-eyed	fair	-haired	long	-shouldered	straight
-hearted	straight	-hearted	single	-haired	open
-haired	dark	-haired	dark	-haired	blue
-haired	broad	-handed	pig	-handed	hard
-eyed	fair	-headed	long	-headed	open
-skinned	hard	-hearted	short	-hearted	hard
-minded	short	-eyed	light	-shouldered	single
-headed	long	-necked	long	-headed	round
-hearted	fair	-skinned	short	-minded	round
-minded	big	-minded	short	-headed	narrow
-minded	blue	-skinned	fair	-minded	long

8.3

The people's alphabet game

Level

Upper-intermediate
to advanced

Time

30–40 minutes

Aim

To practise the language to describe people's appearance, character, feelings, qualities, movement and speech

Materials

One sheet for each group of four to five students

One dice for each group of four to five students

Two counters (or equivalent) for each student

Dictionaries may be useful

Key vocabulary

Suggested here are words for the first four letters of the alphabet for each category. You and your students will come up with many more possibilities.

Adjective: appearance
attractive, big, curvaceous, dainty

Adjective: character
aggressive, bossy, cautious, delightful

Adjective: how people sometimes feel
awkward, bored, cold, disgusted

Noun: a quality you like in people
ambition, bravery, courage, delicacy

Noun: item of clothing
apron, belt, cap, dress

Verb: how people move
accelerate, bolt, crawl, dash

Verb: how people speak
apologise, boast, complain, declare

Warm-up

1   Write on the board the seven categories used on the game board, i.e. *Adjective: appearance, Adjective: character*, etc. Check that students understand these categories.

2   Point to the categories in turn and name any letter of the alphabet. Ask students to think of a word in that category beginning with that letter.

3   Choose one category, e.g. *Verb: how people speak*. Ask students to suggest a word in that category beginning with each letter of the alphabet, excluding X and Z.

Main activity

1   Divide students into groups of four to five. Give each group a dice and the sheet. Each player needs two counters (e.g. coins).

2   Playing the game:

   ▸   Students take turns to throw the dice and move their counter along the Game board. If they land on a blank space, play immediately passes to the next player. If their space has words, they throw the dice again and move their other counter along the Letter board, starting at AB. They have to name something in the category where they landed on the Game board, beginning with one of the letters where they landed on the Letter board.

   ▸   If the player cannot name something they miss a turn.

   ▸   Players may not use a word more than once in any one game.

   ▸   One student in the group lists all the words, by category, named by their group. This student also notes down the categories and letters which made players miss a turn.

   ▸   The first person to reach the end is the winner.

Variations

●   Simplify the game by allowing students to play in pairs, one pair versus another pair, and to use a dictionary to help them find appropriate words.

●   To make the game more competitive, if a player cannot name a word, then the other players may suggest an answer. The first player to name an appropriate word can move their counter forward to the next blank square.

Follow-ups

●   Ask students which categories and letters caused players to miss turns. Find some answers for such combinations with the whole class.

●   Ask students to choose a word they used in the activity. Then ask them to act their word for the rest of the class to guess.

Homework

A   Write a paragraph describing someone you know. Use at least two words from each category in the board game.

B   Find a description of someone from an English-language novel. Write 150 words commenting on how good the description is and why.

Game board

64 **END**	63 **Noun** a quality you like in people	62 **Adjective** appearance	61	60 **Verb** how people speak	59 **Adjective** how people sometimes feel	58 **Verb** how people move	57 **Noun** item of clothing
49 **Adjective** character	50 **Verb** how people speak	51 **Adjective** appearance	52	53 **Noun** a quality you like in people	54	55 **Verb** how people move	56 **Noun** item of clothing
48	47 **Verb** how people speak	46 **Noun** a quality you like in people	45 **Noun** item of clothing	44 **Adjective** how people sometimes feel	43 **Verb** how people move	42 **Adjective** character	41
33 **Verb** how people move	34 **Adjective** how people sometimes feel	35 **Verb** how people speak	36 **Noun** item of clothing	37 **Adjective** appearance	38	39 **Adjective** character	40
32	31 **Adjective** character	30	29 **Adjective** appearance	28 **Noun** a quality you like in people	27 **Verb** how people move	26 **Adjective** how people sometimes feel	25 **Noun** item of clothing
17 **Adjective** how people sometimes feel	18	19 **Noun** item of clothing	20 **Noun** a quality you like in people	21 **Verb** how people move	22 **Adjective** appearance	23 **Verb** how people speak	24
16	15 **Verb** how people move	14 **Adjective** how people sometimes feel	13 **Verb** how people speak	12 **Noun** a quality you like in people	11 **Adjective** appearance	10	9 **Adjective** character
1 **START**	2 **Adjective** appearance	3 **Noun** a quality you like in people	4 **Noun** item of clothing	5	6 **Adjective** character	7 **Adjective** how people sometimes feel	8 **Verb** how people speak

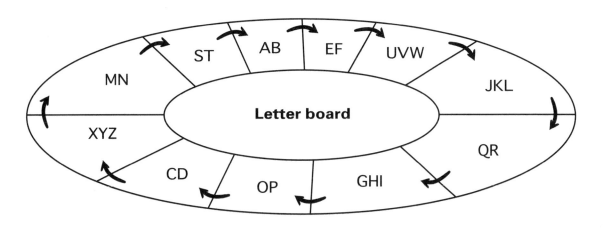

Letter board

MN ST AB EF UVW JKL QR GHI OP CD XYZ

UNIT 9 Describing things

9.1 Everyday objects

Level

Elementary

Time

35–40 minutes

Aim

To practise identifying everyday objects either by their names or by a description of their use

Materials

For Warm-up, one copy of the sheet for each student

For Warm-up (optional), ten or more everyday objects and a coat or cloth to cover them

One set of picture cards, cut up, for each student and for the teacher

One set of 12 counters (or equivalent) for each student

Key vocabulary

alarm clock
blanket
camera
comb
envelope
hairdryer
key
map
mirror
mobile phone
needle and thread
plaster
postcard
purse
safety pin
shampoo
stamp
sun cream
sunglasses
toothbrush
torch
towel
umbrella
watch

Warm-up

1 Divide students into pairs and give each student a copy of the sheet.
2 Ask pairs to match the descriptions with the pictures. Check answers with the whole class and elicit the names of the objects. Write up any new vocabulary on the board.
3 Tell students they have one minute to look at the sheet and remember as many pictures as possible. They should not write anything during this time. After one minute, students turn over their sheets and, in pairs, write down as many words as possible. Check answers and see which pair correctly remembered the most words.

Note: You may wish to bring in real objects for the Warm-up. For step 3, place ten or more objects on a table that all students can see. Allow them one minute to memorise the objects, before you cover them with a cloth or coat. The students then have to write down the objects they remember.

Main activity

1 Give each student a set of picture cards, cut up.
2 Ask each student to choose any 16 of the cards and lay them out in four rows of four in front of them. The cards can be in any order. Make sure each student also has about 12 counters, these can be coins or small pieces of paper.
3 One by one pick cards from your set of pictures and give short descriptions of what each object is used for. If a student has a picture of that object in front of them, they put a counter on the picture. The first student to complete a vertical, diagonal or horizontal row of counters is the winner.
4 You can play the game as many times as you like.

Variations

● For an easier version of this game, simply name the objects instead of describing them.
● Play the game in groups, with one student picking and describing the cards.

Follow-up

Divide students into pairs. Students take turns to pick a card from their set and describe it to their partner. Their partner has to guess the name of the object.

Homework

A Think of six more everyday objects and write a description of each one. Bring your descriptions to the next class and see if your classmates can guess what the objects are.
B Choose six of the objects from the sheet and write a different description for each one.

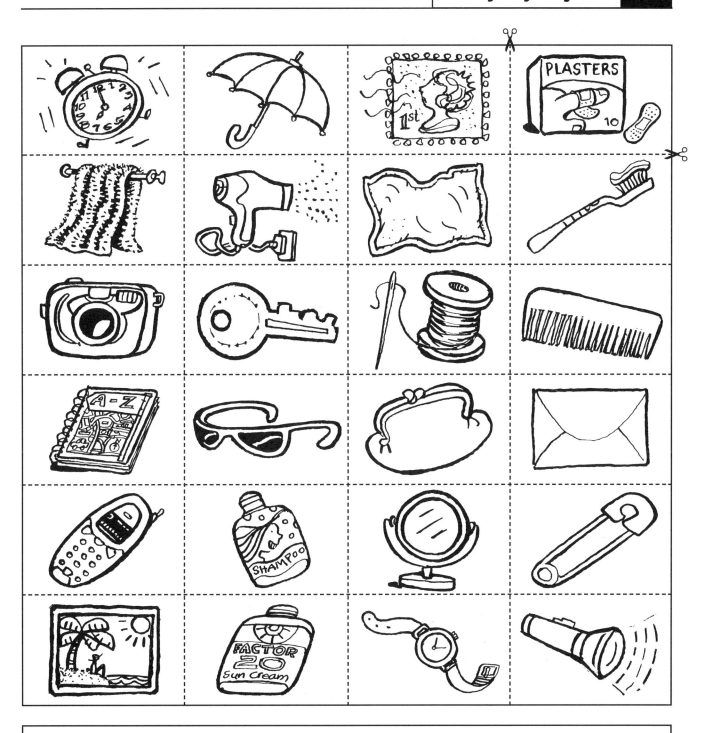

1 a thing that wakes you up in the morning	13 a thing you use to see in the dark
2 a thing for fastening things together	14 something you wash your hair with
3 a thing you put on your skin over a cut	15 a thing you look at yourself with
4 a thing you open the door with	16 a thing you put a letter in
5 a thing you dry your hair with	17 a thing you use for talking to people
6 a thing you put on your bed	18 a thing you wear on your wrist
7 a thing you keep money in	19 a thing you need when it rains
8 a thing you clean your teeth with	20 something you put on your skin in the sun
9 a thing you take pictures with	21 things for repairing clothes
10 a thing you dry yourself with	22 a thing that shows you where to go
11 a thing you write on holiday	23 a thing you put on an envelope
12 a thing you tidy your hair with	24 things you wear over your eyes when it's sunny

9.2

Kim's game

Level

Intermediate

Time

40–45 minutes

Aim

To practise vocabulary of everyday objects and their descriptions

Materials

For Warm-up and Main activity, one copy of the sheet for each student

For Variation (optional), objects that approximately correspond to about ten of the objects on the sheet, and a cloth or coat

For Follow-up, one set of cards, cut up, for each student

Key vocabulary

baseball cap
blade
blunt
broken
buckle
buttons
chewed
chipped
circular
corkscrew
cover
cracked cup
diamond ring
dog-eared
dolphin
frame
half-empty
half-full
high-heeled
laces
logo
missing
oval
padlock and chain
pencil case
penknife
plain
rectangular
rose
rubber
sandal
shabby
spots
stamped addressed
stem
stone
strap
stripes
torn
transparent
zip

Warm-up

1 Give a copy of the sheet to each student.
2 Elicit a description of each object from the students. Try to elicit the words from the Key vocabulary section, although your students may come up with additional points of detail. Write any new vocabulary on the board.

Main activity

1 Ask students to look at the sheet carefully for one minute and try to remember where the objects are on it. After one minute collect the sheets.
2 Divide students into pairs. Tell them to divide a blank page into twenty squares, four across and five down, and to label the columns *A, B, C, D* and the rows *1, 2, 3, 4, 5*.
3 Ask pairs to note on their grid where each item was by writing down the name of the object and any descriptive notes about the object, e.g. *cracked cup with a picture of rose on it* (written in square *1A* of their sheet). They should describe, not draw, the objects.
4 Stop the students after five minutes and check how many items they have remembered.
5 Give students one point for each item in the correct place, e.g. one point for *cup* in the top left-hand corner. Give them an additional point for each detail of description that they wrote, e.g. an extra point for *cracked* and another extra point for *with a picture of a rose on it*.
6 Pairs total their scores to see which pair got the best score.

Variation

Bring in as many objects that correspond to the pictures on the sheet as possible. It is not necessary to find all the objects – ten would be enough. It is also not necessary to have identical objects – your cracked cup might have a different picture on it, for example. After doing the Warm-up activity, show your students your objects and elicit how they differ. Then place your objects in a specific order on a table or tray that all the students can see. Ask them to memorise the order. Then cover the objects with a blanket or coat and ask the students in pairs, or individually as preferred, to write down where and what the objects were. Stop after about five minutes and give points as in the Main activity above.

Follow-up

1 Give each student a set of cards.
2 Divide students into pairs and ask them to sit back to back with a table or flat surface in front of them so that they cannot see each other's cards.
3 Tell Student A to arrange their cards in five rows in any order they like. Student B may then look at the cards for ten seconds. After this Student B must turn round and try to arrange their cards in exactly the same order. They may ask their partner questions to help them with the ones they cannot remember, e.g. *Where's the chipped mug?* When Student B has found the correct order, it is their turn to arrange their cards for Student A.

Homework

A Write descriptions of the objects on the sheet but this time change one aspect of the description, e.g. *a cracked cup with a picture of a bird on it.* In the next lesson show your description to a partner who has to identify what the differences are between your descriptions and the original pictures.
B Cut out ten pictures of objects from a magazine and stick them in rows on a sheet of paper to make a new Kim's game for your class to play. On a separate sheet, write a brief description of each object in the same place as on the sheet you have made. Use your sheet of pictures in another lesson to play Kim's game again with a group of students. Go through the vocabulary for describing your objects before you play the game.

9.3 Name this thing

Level

Upper-intermediate
to advanced

Time

35–45 minutes

Aim

To understand and practise
vocabulary for describing
objects

Materials

One copy of the sheet for each
group of three to four students

One counter (or equivalent) for
each student

For Homework B, a copy of the
sheet for each student

Key vocabulary

A thing with a:
*button, frame, handle, plug,
screen*

A thing made of:
*cloth, glass, leather, metal,
plastic, rubber, wood*

A thing which is:
*heavy, light, prickly, rough,
shiny, smooth, sticky*

A thing which you:
pull, push, squeeze, turn

A thing which:
*bounces, hums, melts, rattles,
rings, spins, tears*

Warm-up

1 Draw a table with five columns and write the following headings at the top of each column:
a thing with a …, a thing made of …, a thing which is …, a thing which you …, a thing which … .
Ask students to copy the table, leaving enough room for up to ten words under each heading.

2 Say a word from the Key vocabulary. Elicit its meaning or demonstrate as necessary. Then ask
students to tell you which heading it belongs under and write it in the correct column.

3 Do the same for all the Key vocabulary, introducing the words in random order. Spend a couple of
minutes brainstorming with the whole class objects for the various words, e.g. things with a screen,
things with a handle, etc.

Main activity

1 Divide students into groups of three or four and give each group a copy of the sheet. Make sure
that each student has a counter, or equivalent.

2 Playing the game:
  ‣ Tell each student to place their counter on one of the letter circles marked 'start'.
  ‣ Explain that the aim of the game is to move across the board to reach the same letter circle
    marked 'finish'.
  ‣ The first player begins by choosing the hexagon nearest to their letter circle and naming an
    object which matches the description. A player may only move to an adjoining hexagon if they
    can correctly name an object.
  ‣ Players take turns to play. They may move in any direction, but may not move to a hexagon if
    another player is there. If a player cannot name an object, they miss a turn.
  ‣ The first player to reach the finish circle for their letter wins.

3 Monitor and help as necessary and stop the game after an appropriate length of time.

Follow-up

1 Send a student out of the room and ask the class to think of an object. Then bring the student
back into the room. Now the student has to guess what the object is by asking different members
of the class questions using the Key vocabulary. If the student guesses the object, they choose the
next student to go outside. If the student can't guess after asking every student in the class a
question, the class wins.

2 This activity can be played several times with different objects.

Homework

A Write ten more descriptions of objects that could be used in a game like this, e.g. *a thing made
of lycra; a thing which is slimy*. Try to think of as unusual words as possible.

B Write an appropriate thing in each of the spaces on the board. Do not write any word more
than once.

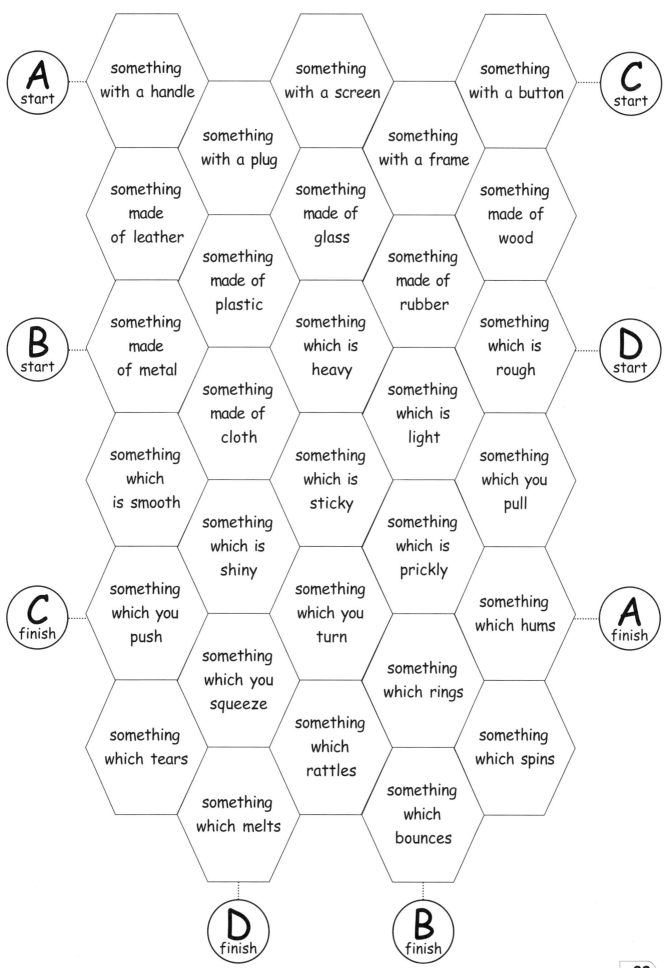

10.1

Poems

Level

Elementary

Time

40–45 minutes

Aim

To practise language for talking about friends

Materials

One copy of the sheet for each student

One sheet of blank paper for each student

Dictionaries may be useful

Key vocabulary

The following words and phrases are used on the sheet but students will probably come up with many other ways of describing people.

afraid of nothing
always smiling
best friend
can sing really well
doesn't get angry
energetic and enthusiastic
friendly
great to be with
happy to help you
honest
intelligent
interested in everything
is always with me
jokes a lot
jolly
kind and friendly
lovely
loves football
makes you feel good
never angry
never nasty
nice and kind
one of the best
open-hearted
original
party animal
quick to help you
reads all the time
sometimes sad
sweet
talks a lot
thinks of others
understanding
unselfish and untidy
very good at art
will always be there for you
xylophone player
young at heart
zestful

Warm-up

1 Put an example of the kind of poem used in this activity on the board. Use the example below for the name Thomas, or create an example using the name of someone you or the class knows.

_ all and handsome
_ appy smile
_ ptimistic
_ akes me laugh
_ lways helpful
_ peaks good English

_ _ _ _ _ _

2 Don't explain the format. Help the class to work it out. They have to find the missing first letter of each line. These spell a name. The name is the last line of the poem.

3 Ask students to suggest alternative words or phrases for each of the letters in the name chosen, e.g. **t**alks a lot, **h**as blue eyes, etc.

Main activity

1 Give each student a copy of the sheet. They work out individually who the three poems are about. Check answers with the whole class.
   Answers *1 Anita 2 Louise 3 John*

2 Divide the students into pairs and ask them to complete the other phrases on the sheet. Clue: they need to use each letter of the alphabet once. See Key vocabulary for the answers.

3 Discuss how some of the phrases could be varied, e.g. *always* could be followed by *happy, friendly, kind, helpful* or *smiling*.

4 Give each student a piece of blank paper and tell them to write their first name at the top. Then collect the papers and give one to each student.

5 Tell students to write a poem like the ones on the sheet for the person whose name is on their piece of paper. They should not leave the initial letters blank. Encourage them to use their own phrases as well as the ones on the sheet. Monitor and help as required.

6 Students give their poems to the people they wrote about. If any students finish earlier than the rest, ask them to swap pages with each other and write a new poem.

Variation

1 Follow steps 1 to 4 above.

2 Then ask students to write a poem for the name they receive, leaving the first letter blank and then folding the top of the paper over so the name is not visible.

3 Collect and number the sheets, then pin them up round the classroom. Students write a list of the numbers in their notebooks. They read the poems and write a name against each number when they identify who each poem is about.

4 Check answers with the whole class.

Follow-up

Choose a person the students all know – perhaps a film star or a sports personality. Pairs then write a poem about that person. Compare what pairs wrote for each letter of the name and ask the class to choose which seems to be the most appropriate phrase for each letter. In this way they build up a new poem, using lines thought up by different pairs of students.

Homework

A Write a poem about yourself or someone else in your family.

B Write a poem about someone else in the class but provide two or three alternative suggestions for each letter. Show the poem to the student and ask them to choose which of the lines to use.

1

__ fraid of nothing

__ ice and kind

__ nterested in everything

__ alks a lot

__ lways fun

— — — — —

2

__ ovely

__ riginal

__ nderstanding

__ ntelligent

__ weet

__ nthusiastic

— — — — — —

3

__ olly

__ pen-hearted

__ onest

__ ever nasty

— — — —

Here are some phrases that might help you write some puzzle poems.

__ akes you feel good

__ an sing really well

__ appy to help you

__ arty animal

__ eads all the time

__ estful

__ ery good at art

__ est friend

__ ever angry

__ hinks of others

__ ill always be there for you

__ lways smiling

__ ne of the best

__ nselfish and untidy

__ oesn't get cross

__ ometimes sad

__ oves football

__ reat to be with

__ riendly

__ s always with me

__ ylophone player

__ uick to help you

__ nergetic and enthusiastic

__ ind and friendly

__ okes a lot

__ oung at heart

10.2 Interesting people

Level

Intermediate

Time

40–45 minutes

Aim

To practise language for talking about people's lives and backgrounds

Materials

For Warm-up, a picture of a person that the students will all be able to see

One set of pictures and questions, cut up, for each group of four to six students

One dice for each group of four to six students

For Homework B, a copy of the sheet, not cut up, for each student

Key vocabulary

afraid of
ambition
best friend
characteristic
colleagues
enjoy
favourite
happen
item of clothing
neighbours
parent
proudest moment
regret
relationship
romantic life
secret
spend time
typically
upset
win a million dollars

The activity should also activate a lot of other vocabulary in this topic area.

Warm-up

1 Show the class a picture of a person that the class can all see.
2 Ask the class questions about that person – name, age, marital status, family, home, job, ambitions, fears, likes and dislikes, etc. Encourage the class to use their imagination. If there are any questions on the photocopiable sheet that you think your students may have difficulty with, practise those questions too.

Main activity

1 Divide students into groups of four to six. Give each group a set of pictures and question cards. Groups spread the pictures out face up in front of them. They place the question cards in a pile face down on the table.
2 Each student takes turns to throw the dice. If they throw a 3, for example, they look at picture 3 and say what that person's name is, their age, marital status and whether they have any children.
3 If the next player throws a different number, they give the name, age, marital status and children for the picture with that number. If they throw the same number as the first player, they repeat the basic information that the first player gave but they also turn over a question card and answer that question about that person. They leave the question card beside that picture.
4 Play continues like this until all the questions have been used. Each time a player will either be giving information about a new picture or will be repeating all the information previously given about a picture and adding more information based on a new question. The other students can help them if they cannot remember all the information previously given.

Variation

Divide the students into groups of six or fewer. Each student in the group takes one of the pictures and is the only person to talk about that character. Students take turns to pick a question card and read it out. They then throw the dice and the person who has the picture with that number must answer the question. Where the group has only two or three students, each student can take two or three pictures. If there are four to five students, they can throw the dice until the number thrown corresponds to a student's picture.

Follow-up

Ask students to stay in the same groups. Tell them to shuffle the question cards and place them in a pile face down. Students take turns to pick a card and ask the question to the person on their left. The student should reword the question to read 'you' rather than 'they'.

Homework

A Choose one character that your group worked with. Write what that person might write in a letter or write on their old school website, telling former school friends what they have been doing since leaving school. Use as much language from the activity as possible.
B Choose one of the characters. Write an interview with the character you chose using some of the questions that were not answered by that character during the main activity.

Acknowledgement
The idea for this game was inspired by a session given at IATEFL 2001 by Anthea Home, EFL Games (www.eflgames.com), Switzerland.

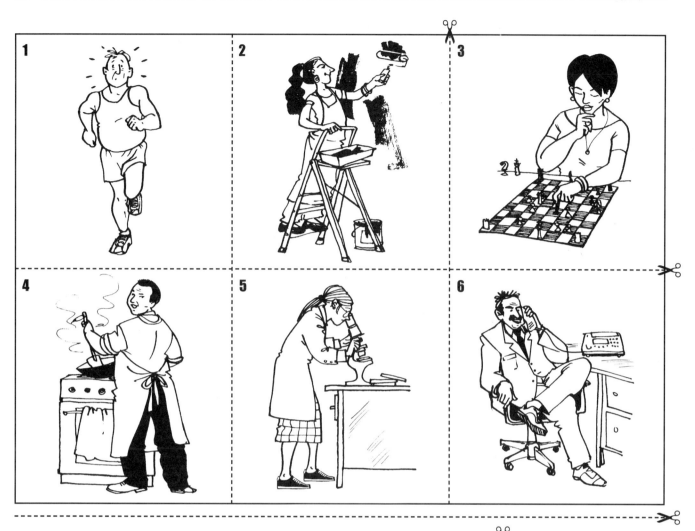

| 1 | 2 | 3 |
| 4 | 5 | 6 |

What's their favourite music and where do they listen to it?	What's their greatest ambition?	What's the worst thing that has ever happened to them?	What has been their proudest moment?
Where did they spend their last holiday?	What exactly is their job and how do they feel about it?	What's their relationship like with their neighbours?	How do they feel about their colleagues?
What kind of car do they drive?	Who's their best friend? How did they meet and how do they now spend time together?	What secret do they have in their lives?	What's their main regret?
What do they enjoy doing most?	How do they typically spend their weekends?	How did they spend their last birthday?	What do they like to read?
What are they most afraid of?	How would you describe their home?	What's their best characteristic and what's their worst characteristic?	What's their favourite food?
If they won a million dollars, what would they spend it on?	What's their favourite item of clothing?	What do they do when they are upset?	What kind of parent are they, or would they be?

UNIT 10 Friends and relationships

Feelings

Level

Upper–intermediate
to advanced

Time

40–45 minutes

Aim

To practise talking about the
language of feelings

Materials

One copy of the sheet, cut up,
for each group of four to five
players

Note: you may wish to remove
some words which are not
relevant or add your own in the
blank squares

One dice for each group of four
to five students

One counter (or equivalent) for
each student

For Follow-up, for the first
Variation and for Homework A,
one copy of the sheet, not cut
up, for each student

Key vocabulary

See photocopiable sheet
opposite

Warm-up

1 Ask students how they feel in different situations, e.g. before an exam, after a holiday. Brainstorm words for feelings on the board.
2 Try to elicit as many words as possible from the Key vocabulary list.

Main activity

1 Divide students into groups of four to five. Give each group a dice and the cut-up sheet. (You can remove some of the adjectives from your students' sets if you feel that they are not relevant or you can add your own in the blank squares.) Each player also needs a counter, e.g. a coin.
2 Students spread out the words face up in rows to make a board.
3 In turn, students put their counters anywhere on their board. They must then talk about a situation when they have felt or would feel that way, e.g. *I felt thrilled when I learnt that I had won a prize in the poetry competition* or *I would feel upset if a friend or a member of my family lost their job.*
4 In turn, students then throw the dice and move their counter the number of spaces indicated. They may move in any direction but must then talk about the feeling they land on.
5 If students land on a square that they have already talked about, a new example situation must be found for that feeling.
6 Play continues until each player has had eight to ten chances to describe their feelings.

Variations

*   Do not cut up the sheet. Students start at any point they wish on it and move round the board in alphabetical order, moving their counter straight back to *annoyed* when they get to *upset*. Follow points 5 and 6 above.
*   This variation is a different game with the same cards:
    1 Choose the same number of cards as there are students in the class and write the words from these cards on the board. Meanwhile, students write the names of all the members of the class on a piece of paper.
    2 Give each student a card. Students look at their card and then give it back.
    3 Explain that students are going to have a party where they should speak and act according to the feeling on their card. Assign one student to be the host of the party. Students move around the classroom chatting to other students as they might at a party but trying to show that they are, say, Mr Efficient or Ms Glamorous.
    4 When students think that they know which characteristic goes with which student, they should write it down on their paper. They can use the words on the board from the Warm-up to help them.
    5 Stop after ten minutes and check who was identified correctly.

Follow-up

Ask students to write one of these adverbs – *usually, often, sometimes, hardly ever, never* – beside each word on the sheet, depending on how often they experience that feeling. They then compare their answers with a partner, discussing ones where they chose a very different adverb.

Homework

A Choose six words from the sheet that best describe how you have felt during the last week. Write a paragraph using these words to describe when and why you had these feelings.
B Divide the adjectives on the sheet into pairs of opposites. If you cannot find an opposite on the sheet, think of a new adjective to make a pair.

Acknowledgement
The idea for this game was inspired by a session given at IATEFL 2001 by Anthea Home, EFL Games
(www.eflgames.com), Switzerland.

upset	uncomfortable	thrilled	tense	tender
sensitive	shocked	shy	sick	suspicious
scornful	scared	satisfied	romantic	resentful
proud	refreshed	relaxed	relieved	reluctant
passionate	optimistic	numb	miserable	lonely
homesick	impatient	indecisive	jealous	lethargic
helpless	guilty	grateful	glamorous	furious
exhilarated	fascinated	fed up	foolish	frustrated
exhausted	excited	envious	embarrassed	efficient
disappointed	disgusted	dissatisfied	dizzy	ecstatic
confused	confident	comfortable	cheerful	brave
annoyed	apprehensive	ashamed	astonished	bored

11.1

Describing the body

Level

Elementary

Time

35–40 minutes

Aim

To practise naming and describing parts of the body

Materials

One copy of Word square A for half the students in the class

One copy of Word square B for half the students in the class

One copy of the body picture and instructions for each student

For Variation, one copy of the sheet, cut up, for each pair of students. You should also cut the clues from the Word squares

Key vocabulary

ankle
arm
back
chest
chin
ear
elbow
eye
finger
foot (feet)
hair
hand
head
heel
knee
leg
mouth
neck
nose
shoulder
stomach
toe
tooth (teeth)
waist
wrist

Warm-up

1 Elicit the Key vocabulary for the parts of the body and write the words on the board.

2 Practise the vocabulary with students by saying each word and pointing to those parts of your body. Ask students to stand up and copy what you are doing. Then point without speaking and encourage students to say the word.

3 Practise the plural forms of the Key vocabulary where appropriate, paying particular attention to *foot/feet*, *tooth/teeth* and *hair/hair*.

Main activity

1 Divide the class into two groups, A and B. Give each student in group A a copy of Word square A and each student in group B a copy of Word square B. Wipe any Key vocabulary from the Warm-up off the board.

2 Ask students to work with another person in their group. Together they find the 12 words hidden in their Word square, using the clues. Each word is the name of a part of the body. Monitor and check as necessary.

3 When students have found all the words, regroup the class so that a student with Word square A is paired with a student with Word square B.

4 Give each student a copy of the body picture and instructions. Read through the instructions on the sheet with the whole class and check that they understand the task.

5 When pairs have completed their sheets, check answers with the whole class.

Answers

A 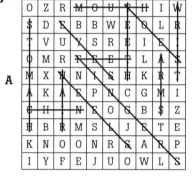 B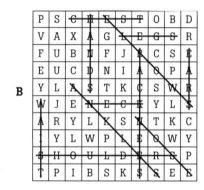

Variation

Students work in pairs. One student in each pair has one of the Word squares and the other has the clues for that Word square. The student with the clues read them one by one and the student with the Word square must find the appropriate word for each clue. The first pair to find the words to match all the clues in the Word square is the winner. This should then be repeated with the other Word square, before students then look at the body sheet.

Follow-up

Allow students one minute to individually write down as many of the words for parts of the body that they remember from the activity. Then in pairs they compare their lists and count how many different words they remembered between them. Find out which pair wrote down most words.

Homework

A Make a new Word square with as many of the words from the activity as possible. Keep a note of all the words you managed to include in your square. Bring it to the next class for another student or pair of students to find the words in it.

B Find three more words for different parts of the body. Write clues for the words and bring them to the next class.

Word square A

O	Z	R	M	O	U	T	H	I	W
S	D	E	B	B	W	E	O	L	R
T	V	U	Y	S	R	E	I	E	I
O	M	R	F	E	E	T	L	A	S
M	X	H	N	I	S	H	K	R	T
A	K	A	E	P	N	C	G	M	I
C	H	I	N	E	O	G	B	S	Z
H	B	R	M	S	L	J	E	T	E
K	N	O	O	N	R	S	A	R	P
I	Y	F	E	J	U	O	W	L	S

Find these words in square A:

- you put your food into this
- you have ten on your feet
- you wear your watch around this
- you should brush these after meals
- you see with these
- these are at the ends of your legs
- you have ten on your hands
- most people have this on their head
- when you are hungry, this makes strange noises
- this part of your face is between your mouth and your neck
- these are between your shoulders and your hands
- these are the back parts of your feet

Word square B

P	S	C	H	E	S	T	O	B	D
V	A	X	A	G	L	E	G	S	R
F	U	B	N	F	J	B	C	S	E
E	U	C	D	N	I	A	O	P	A
Y	L	A	S	T	K	C	S	W	R
W	J	E	N	E	C	K	Y	L	S
A	R	Y	L	K	S	N	T	K	C
I	Y	L	W	P	L	E	O	W	Y
S	H	O	U	L	D	E	R	S	P
T	P	I	B	S	K	S	S	E	E

Find these words in square B:

- you hear with these
- these are where your arms bend
- these are at the ends of your arms
- you smell things with this
- these are between your arms and the main part of your body
- you use these for walking
- this gets bigger if you eat too much
- you lie on this when you are in bed
- this moves in and out when you breathe
- these are in the middle of your legs
- the collar of your shirt fits round here
- these join your feet to your legs

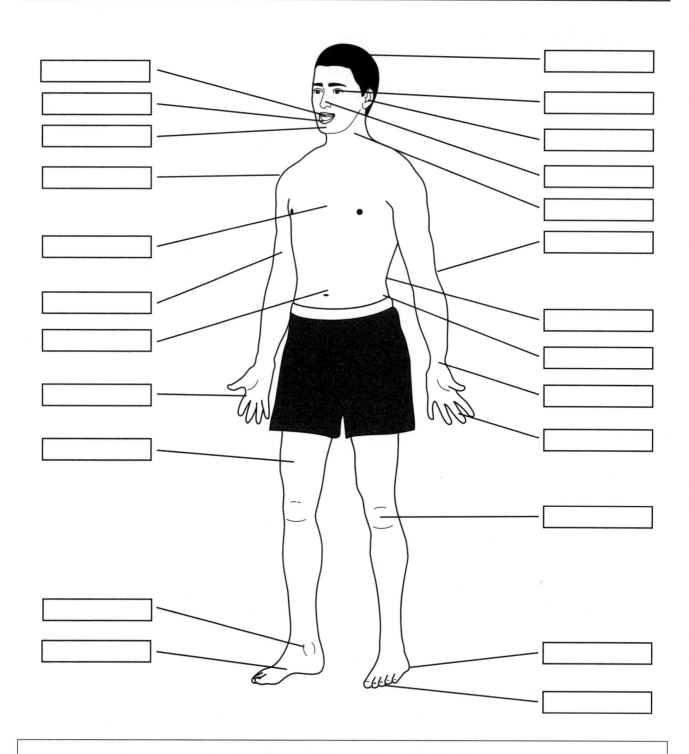

Instructions – Describing the body

Student A:

Read a clue from your Word square.

Student B:

Try to name the word.

If you don't know the answer, ask your partner to tell you.

Then write the correct word in the box.

Take turns to read your clues until you have filled in all the words on the picture.

11.2

Doctor, doctor

Level

Intermediate

Time

45 minutes for Main activity; you may wish to do the Warm-up in a previous lesson

Aim

To practise vocabulary related to everyday illnesses, their symptoms and treatments

Materials

Sticky labels for each student

One Patient card for each patient

One Doctor's treatment card for each doctor

One copy of the Patient instructions for each patient

One copy of the Doctor instructions for each doctor

For Follow-up, six sticky gold or silver stars (or equivalent) for each patient

Key vocabulary

Symptoms:
be itchy
catch a cold
have a cough
have a headache
have a high temperature
have a rash
have a sore throat
have backache
have insomnia
have stomach ache
lose weight
put on weight
rub
scratch
sneeze
sprain
suffer from stress

Treatments:
antibiotics
bandage
cough mixture
cream
diet
exercise
go to hospital for some tests
have an operation
I'll give you a prescription for ...
injection
painkillers
physiotherapy
stitches
tablets
vitamins
X-ray

Warm-up

1   Ask the class to brainstorm reasons why someone might go to see the doctor. Make a list on the board of the problems and symptoms, focusing on the Key vocabulary.

2   Ask students to discuss in pairs ways of treating each of the problems. Then discuss as a whole class the treatments, eliciting the Key vocabulary.

3   Tell students to imagine that they are at the doctor's surgery and try to elicit a typical dialogue from them. Write up the key phrases on the board, e.g.
Doctor: *Good morning. How can I help you?*
Patient: *I've got a rash on my arm.*
Doctor: *How long have you had it?*
Patient: *About two days.*
Doctor: *I'll give you a prescription for some cream.*
Patient: *Thank you, Doctor. Goodbye.*
Ask students to practise the dialogue in pairs and substitute different health problems and treatments.

Main activity

1   Divide the class into two equal groups; one group of doctors and one group of patients.

2   Arrange the classroom so that each doctor has a surgery behind a desk, with a chair in front of it, and make one part of the classroom the waiting room.

3   Give a sticky label to each doctor and each patient. Ask them to choose a name, write it on the label, and wear it as a badge.

4   Give each patient one of the Patient cards and the Patient instructions, and give each doctor a Doctor's treatment card and the Doctor instructions.

5   Go through the instructions sheet with the whole class and check that they understand the task.

6   Allow students to do the role plays and stop the activity after an appropriate time.

Variation

For small groups, put the Patient cards face down in a pile on the doctor's desk. The patient students pick a card when they visit the doctor. After the doctor has suggested a treatment, the patient goes to another doctor and picks a new card from the pile on the doctor's table.

Follow-up

1   Give each patient six stars to be awarded to the doctors as follows: three stars for the most helpful doctor, two stars for the second best, one star for the third best.

2   Students go and stick the stars on the doctors' name badges. If you do not have star stickers, you can write the doctors' names on the board and write up the number of stars the students award to each doctor. Ask students to explain to the class why they awarded stars as they did.

3   Ask the doctors which patients were the easiest and which were the most difficult to deal with.

Homework

A   Write a list of six common medical problems and the possible treatments for them.

B   Make a list of the things that it is useful to have in a first-aid cabinet at home, explaining why each thing is useful.

Doctor's treatment card

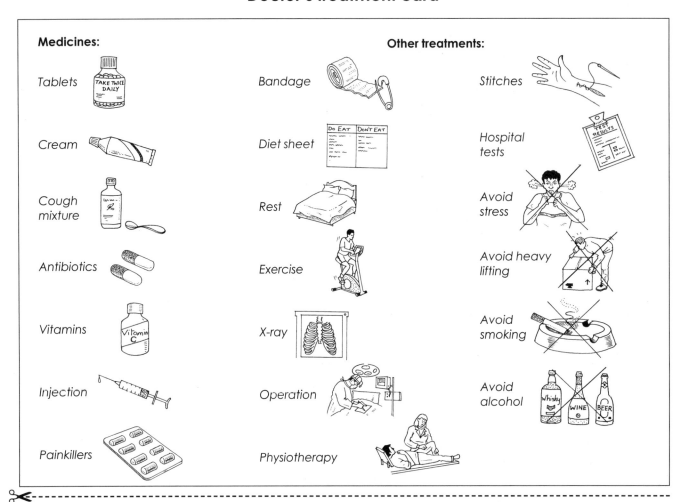

Medicines:

Tablets

Cream

Cough mixture

Antibiotics

Vitamins

Injection

Painkillers

Other treatments:

Bandage

Diet sheet

Rest

Exercise

X-ray

Operation

Physiotherapy

Stitches

Hospital tests

Avoid stress

Avoid heavy lifting

Avoid smoking

Avoid alcohol

Patient cards

"I'm putting on too much weight."

"I've got a headache and my throat is sore."

"I've got an itchy rash on my arm."

"I've cut my finger and it's bleeding a lot."

"I'm tired all the time."

"I've got terrible backache."

"I think I've sprained my ankle."

"I can't get to sleep at night."

Patient instructions

You are not feeling well, and you want some medical advice. You have had bad experiences with doctors in the past, so you decide to visit three different doctors to see who will give you the best treatment for your problem.
You should wait in the waiting room until a doctor is free to see you.

The doctor will ask you:

- **what your problem is**
- **how long you have had the problem**
- **what you think caused it**

You should answer the questions with as much detail as possible.

After each visit you should return to the waiting room.
When you have seen three different doctors, you should decide which is the best doctor and why.

Doctor instructions

A number of patients are waiting to see you with different problems. They will ask you to help them.
The patients are waiting in the waiting room. When you are free, you should call a patient into your surgery.

Ask the patient:

- **what their problem is** *(What can I do for you? What seems to be the trouble?)*
- **how long they have had the problem** *(How long have you had this trouble/problem?)*
- **what they think caused it** *(What do you think caused it?)*

Listen to their answers and then suggest a treatment that will help them.

You will find out later whether each patient was satisfied with the advice you gave them.

11.3

Idioms of the body

Level

Upper-intermediate
to advanced

Time

40–45 minutes

Aims

To introduce and practise
idioms which include parts of
the body

Materials

For Warm-up, one set of Idiom
cards and one set of Definition
cards, cut up, for each pair of
students

One set of Idiom cards and one
set of Definition cards, cut up
and combined, for each group
of six to eight students

One copy of the sheet, not cut
up, for each group of six to
eight students. The idioms
should be numbered 1–30 and
the definition for each idiom
should be numbered
correspondingly.

Dictionaries may be useful

Key vocabulary

See photocopiable sheet
opposite

Warm-up

1   Write these six parts of the body on the board: *head, face, hand, eye, finger, foot* and then write
one of the idioms on the board. Try to elicit the meaning of the idiom and ask students if they
know any other idioms containing any of those words for parts of the body.

2   Divide the students into pairs. Give each pair a set of Idiom cards and a set of Definition cards. Ask
the students to match each idiom with its definition.

3   Check answers with the whole class. Collect the sets of cards.

Main activity

1   Divide the class into groups of six to eight students. Ask them to sit around a table and give each
group a set of Idiom cards and Definition cards.

2   Give one person in each group a copy of the answer sheet you have prepared. The idioms should
be numbered 1–30 and the answer definitions numbered correspondingly. This student will be
the referee during the game and should not show the sheet to the group.

3   Ask groups to divide their cards into two piles – idioms and definitions. They should place each
pile face down on the table.

4   Tell students to take turns to pick up one card from the top of each pile. To win points the student
has to try to do the following two things:
    a) For one point, give the part of the body in the idiom that matches the definition card they
        picked. For an additional point, correctly give the whole idiom that matches the definition.
    b) For one point, explain the meaning of the idiom card picked.
    If a student is lucky enough to pick a matching idiom and definition, they get four points.
    The referee with the numbered answer sheet records the scores for the group. You may want
    to write the key points of the scoring system on the board to help students.

5   When cards have been used, they are returned to the bottom of the pile. If the set of cards has
been completely worked through, both piles are shuffled before continuing the game.

6   The student with the highest score when you stop the game is the winner.

Variation

Students work in groups of six to eight with one pile of cards, i.e. a mixed pile of idioms and
definitions. One student in the group has the numbered answer sheet. Students take turns to pick one
card. If it is a definition card and they can give the correct part of the body from the idiom, they win
one point. They win an extra point if they can give the whole idiom. If it is an idiom card and they can
give the correct definition, they win one point.

Follow-up

1   Divide students into pairs and give each pair one Idiom card.

2   Ask them to think of a situation to present to the class, illustrating how that idiom might be used.
For example, if a pair has *put a brave face on it*, they might give the class the following situation:
*Anne was very upset when she lost her job. However, she didn't want her dad to realise how
worried she was, so when he asked about it, she said that she was sure she would easily get
another job and that she'd never really liked the old job.*

3   Pairs present their situations to the class and the class has to guess the correct idiom.

Homework

A   Look up the words *arm, back, hair, heart, leg, neck, nose* in a good dictionary. Make a note of one
interesting idiom based on each of these words.

B   Write a story with the title *An Extraordinary Day,* using as many as possible of the idioms from the
activity.

Idiom cards

say something off the top of your head	put on a brave face	give someone a hand	keep an eye on something	have a finger in every pie	put your foot in it
put your head on the block	try to keep a straight face	have time on your hands	turn a blind eye	let something slip through your fingers	start off on the wrong foot
keep your head	save face	have a free hand	need eyes in the back of your head	cross your fingers	stand on your own feet
do something standing on your head	pull a face	live from hand to mouth	be up to your eyes in something	have your finger on the pulse	get itchy feet
bury your head in the sand	come face to face with someone	have your hands full	pull the wool over someone's eyes	put your finger on something	put your foot down

Definition cards

say the first thing that you think of	try not to show that you are unhappy	help someone	watch to make sure if something is safe	be involved in many different activities	say the wrong thing and feel embarrassed
take a big risk which may damage your position	do your best not to smile or laugh	have too little to do	pretend not to see something	miss an opportunity	make a bad start when meeting someone new
stay calm and in control	protect yourself from being embarrassed	be able to make your own decisions	need to be watching in all directions	hope that everything will work out well	be independent and not rely on other people
do something very easily, without needing to think about it	show dislike or disgust	have very little money to live on	be very busy	know all the latest news and what is happening	want to travel or to move on to something new
pretend that something isn't happening	suddenly meet someone by chance	be very busy	deliberately mislead someone	see exactly what the problem is, or what the answer is	assert your authority

12.1

Mystery evening out

Level

Elementary

Time

30–35 minutes

Aim

To practise talking about an evening out in an entertaining way

Materials

One copy of the sheet, cut up, for each student

Key vocabulary

Adjectives describing people
e.g. *beautiful, clever, tall, thin*

Leisure activities
e.g. *jogging, playing the guitar, swimming*

Noun
e.g. *bicycle, hat, horse*

Adjectives describing a film
e.g. *exciting, funny, interesting*

Food
e.g. *apple, chips, rice*

Drink
e.g. *milk, orange juice, water*

Question
e.g. *Do you love me? What's your name?*

Answer
e.g. *Black, without sugar. It's half past six.*

Verbs in past tense
e.g. *danced, ran, swam, talked*

Adjectives describing how you can feel
e.g. *bored, cold, happy*

Odd number
e.g. *1, 3, 5*
Even number
e.g. *2, 4, 6*

Warm-up

1 Write on the board the ten categories from the Key vocabulary, i.e. *Adjective describing people, Leisure activity*, etc.
2 Ask students to suggest words that fit each category and write them on the board.

Main activity

1 Give each student a Mystery words sheet. Ask them to complete it individually with any words they like. Make sure they write a complete question and answer for numbers 15 and 16 respectively. Monitor and check as necessary.
2 Give each student a Mystery evening out sheet and ask them to write the words they put in the odd numbers (1, 3, 5, etc.) of their Mystery words sheet into the appropriate spaces in their Mystery evening out sheet. Make sure students look carefully at the numbers because numbers 1 and 10 are repeated in the story intentionally.
3 Divide students into pairs and ask them to exchange their Mystery evening out sheets. Then tell them to write their even-numbered words in the remaining boxes (2, 4, 6, etc.).
4 In pairs, students take turns to read each other the story on the sheet they have. Pairs discuss which of their two stories they thought was the better one.

Follow-up

Each pair reads the better of their two stories out to the rest of the class. The class then votes on the best story.

Homework

A Redraft the story you created in class. Keep the same people, but try and make the rest of the story more realistic.
B Write a paragraph about a real evening out.

Mystery words

The name of a man (someone the class knows, e.g. *a film star* or *a member of the class*):

1 ....

Two adjectives that can be used to describe a person:

2 ....   3 ....

Two leisure activities: 4 ....   5 ....

A number: 6 ....

A noun: 7 ....

Two adjectives describing a film: 8 ....   9 ....

The name of a woman (someone the class knows, e.g. *a film star* or *a member of the class*):

10 ....

Two more adjectives describing a person:

11 ....   12 ....

A type of food: 13 ....

A type of drink: 14 ....

A question: 15 ....

An answer: 16 ....

A place where you can go in your spare time: 17 ....

Two things you did last weekend (with verbs in the past tense):

18 ....   19 ....

An adjective describing how you can feel: 20 ....

Mystery evening out

Last night I went to the cinema with (1).......................... . I like him because he is very
(2).......................... and (3).......................... . He is very good at (4).......................... but he
is terrible at (5).......................... . The film was called (6)..........................
(7).......................... . I thought it was (8).......................... but (1)..........................
thought it was (9).......................... .

As we came out of the cinema we met (10).......................... . She looked very
(11).......................... and (12).......................... . We invited her to go to a café with us. We all
ate (13).......................... and drank (14).......................... . After the meal,
(10).......................... asked: (15)".......................... ?"
(1).......................... answered: (16) ".......................... ."

So we decided to go to (17).........................., where we (18).......................... and then
we (19).......................... . As a result, I feel very (20).......................... today.

12.2

Picture your free time

Level

Intermediate

Time

30–35 minutes

Aim

To revise the vocabulary of
leisure activities

Materials

One copy of the sheet, cut up
and put in an envelope

Some blank sheets of paper for
each team of three to four
players

For Follow-up, one copy of the
sheet, not cut up, for each
student

For Homeworks A and B, one
copy of the sheet, not cut up,
for each student

Key vocabulary

People
*disc jockey, goalkeeper,
gymnast, mountaineer, referee,
snooker player,*

Activities
*to dive, to go clubbing, to high
jump, to kick, to paint, to play
squash, to play the violin, to
score a goal, to skate, to
sunbathe, to window-shop*

Things
*baseball bat, binoculars,
bowling alley, camcorder,
chess board, comic book,
computer game, diary, dice,
exercise bike, goggles, golf
club, headphones, helmet,
horror film, in-line skates,
mountain bike, murder mystery
book, orchestra, road map,
satellite dish, skateboard,
speakers, sunglasses,
swimming pool, swimming
trunks, tennis racket, tent*

Warm-up

1 Ask students what they like doing in their leisure time. Encourage them to produce some of the Key vocabulary.
2 Check any items of Key vocabulary that you think the class may not know. Ask questions for some items that you want to check, e.g. *What do you hold in your hand when you play tennis?* (tennis racket). Alternatively, draw simple pictures on the board to elicit other items, e.g. *dice, golf club, beach ball, bottle opener.*

Main activity

1 Divide the class into teams of three or four students and give each team some blank sheets of paper. Tell the teams to write the heading *Guessed Words* on one sheet. The other sheets will be used for drawing pictures. Place the envelope of picture cards on a desk at the front.
2 Playing the game:
  ‣ One person from each team comes to the desk at the front and picks a card. They look at the card and then return it to the envelope.
  ‣ The student goes back to their team and indicates by holding up the appropriate number of fingers how many words were written on their card. The student then draws their own picture to represent what was on the card. The other members of the team have to guess the word(s) from the drawing. The artist may not speak and may only nod or shake their head to indicate yes or no respectively.
  ‣ When the team guesses what was written on the card, the artist writes it down on the *Guessed Words* sheet, while another member of the team picks another card from the envelope. If they pick a card that their team already has, they choose another one. All the members of the team take turns to be the artist.
  ‣ If after one minute the group does not guess the word, the student tells them.
  ‣ Play the game until each student has had at least two turns at being the artist.
  ‣ The winning team is the one which has written down the largest number of guessed words.

Variation

With smaller classes this activity can be played as a whole class. Students take it in turns to pick a card from the envelope. They then draw the item on the board and the other students guess what is being drawn. The first person to guess the drawing correctly gets one point.

Follow-up

Give each student a copy of the sheet, not cut up. Ask them to put the words in groups in any way that seems logical to them. Then ask them to compare and explain their groupings to other students.

Homework

A Write a paragraph about your own leisure activities using as many of the words from the sheet as possible.
B Choose five words or expressions from the sheet and write down three collocations for each of them, e.g. *to borrow/buy/use a tennis racket.*

baseball bat	binoculars	bowling alley	camcorder	chess board
comic book	computer game	diary	dice	disc jockey
to dive	exercise bike	goalkeeper	to go clubbing	goggles
golf club	gymnast	headphones	helmet	high jump
horror film	to kick	mountain bike	mountaineer	murder mystery
orchestra	to paint	to play squash	to play the violin	referee
road map	in-line skates	satellite dish	to score a goal	to skate
skateboard	snooker player	speakers	to sunbathe	sunglasses
swimming pool	swimming trunks	tennis racket	tent	to window-shop

12.3

Can you do any conjuring tricks?

Level

Upper-intermediate
to advanced

Time

40–45 minutes

Aim

To practise talking about leisure
activities

Materials

One copy of the sheet for each
student

For Homework B, a copy of the
sheet for each student

Key vocabulary

See photocopiable sheet
opposite

Warm-up

1 Elicit the leisure activities from the sheet and write them on the board. Alternatively, you could
dictate them to students.

2 Ask students to write down each of the activities in one of the following categories:
Outdoor activities, Indoor pastimes, Arts and crafts.

3 As a whole class, compare how students classified the activities and ask them to justify any
choices that were different from the suggestions below.

Outdoor activities	Indoor pastimes	Arts and crafts
Bungee-jumping	Card games	Cookery
Canoeing	Conjuring	Knitting
Gardening	Pool	Painting (watercolours or oils)
Golf	Salsa dancing	Photography
Hang-gliding	Webpage design	Playing a musical instrument
Kite-flying		Pottery
In-line skating		
Skateboarding		
Skiing		

Main activity

1 Give each student a copy of the sheet and ask them to complete it individually.

2 Divide students into groups of three to four. Ask them to compare how they filled in their sheets
and tell each other about any experiences they have had doing these activities, explaining why
they would or would not like to try them (again).

3 The students who have put ticks in the third column should explain what teaching advice they
would give students in their group who want to learn about that activity.

Variation

Students work in pairs and fill in the sheets for each other by asking each other questions about which
of the activities they have tried and which they would like to try, etc. Encourage students not just to tick
the boxes but to explain the reasons for their answers.

Follow-up

Ask students to mingle and find two or three people who have some of the same ticks in the
... could you teach someone else? column. In these new groups, students should choose just one of
the activities they are good at. If possible, make sure that groups are working on different activities.
Each group should compose a flyer encouraging someone to take up the activity or do a class in it. If
there is time, pin up the flyers around the classroom and ask students to read them and vote on the
most persuasive flyer.

Homework

A Write 150–200 words explaining which of these activities you would be most interested in
learning (more) about and which you would least like to learn (more) about.

B Find someone outside the class and ask them questions to complete the sheet about leisure
activities. If necessary ask them for the information you need in your first language. Then write
150–200 words explaining what you learnt about that person. Describe what experiences they
have had and explain why they would like to learn more about the activities of their choice.

Which of these leisure activities …	… have you tried?	… would you like to learn (more) about?	… could you teach someone else?
Bungee-jumping	○	○	○
Canoeing	○	○	○
Card games	○	○	○
Conjuring	○	○	○
Cookery	○	○	○
Gardening	○	○	○
Golf	○	○	○
Hang-gliding	○	○	○
In-line skating	○	○	○
Kite-flying	○	○	○
Knitting	○	○	○
Painting (watercolours or oils)	○	○	○
Photography	○	○	○
Playing a musical instrument	○	○	○
Pool	○	○	○
Pottery	○	○	○
Salsa dancing	○	○	○
Skateboarding	○	○	○
Skiing	○	○	○
Webpage design	○	○	○

13.1

My first school

Level

Elementary

Time

40–45 minutes

Aim

To practise vocabulary for describing what you remember about your first school

Materials

One copy of Text A for half the students in the class

One copy of Text B for half the students in the class

One enlarged copy each of Texts A and B for the classroom wall; you may need more copies for larger classes

For Variation, one copy of Text A for each pair of students and several enlarged copies of Text B

Sticky tape or drawing pins

Key vocabulary

art, board, book, break, canteen, classroom, clock, corridor, desk, fast, first floor, fond of, frightened of, geography, ground floor, headteacher, history, kind, lesson, map, music, packed lunch, pencil, picture, reading, row, share, slow, strict, teacher, writing

Answers
strict/kind
frightened/fond
first/ground
thirty/twenty
front/back
door/board
slow/fast
reading/writing
book/pencils
half-hour/fifteen-minute
10.30/11 o'clock
art/music
brought a packed lunch/had lunch in the school canteen
geography/history
smiled/laughed
boring/difficult
maps/pictures
listened to cassettes/ watched videos
places/people

Warm-up

1 Ask students to describe the classroom they are in. Write up a list of key classroom objects or furniture on the board.
2 Ask them if their first school classroom was like this one. Discuss similarities and differences.
3 Divide the class into two halves, A and B. Give a copy of Text A to each student in half A, and a copy of Text B to each student in half B. Tell them to read the text with another student from their half of the class and check that they understand it. Monitor and help as necessary.

Main activity

1 Stick an enlarged copy of Text A to one wall of the classroom and an enlarged copy of Text B to another wall. For larger classes you may wish to have more copies on the wall.
2 Divide group A into pairs and divide group B into pairs. Tell the pairs that one of them is the messenger and the other is the scribe (or writer). The scribe should have a copy of their own text in front of them. Explain that the messenger has to run to the wall and look at the other group's text, i.e. an A student goes to look at Text B and vice versa. The messenger is not allowed to have a pen or paper.
3 Explain that there are a number of differences between the two texts, but do not say how many. The messenger has to read the other text on the wall and memorise anything which seems to be different to their text, then go back and tell the scribe. The scribe notes this difference on their text. The messenger then returns to the wall and memorises the next difference, etc. until they think they have found all the differences.
4 When all the pairs have finished, tell the A pairs to find a B pair. Together they check to see how many differences they found.
5 Check answers with the whole class and see which pair found the largest number of differences. The actual number of differences is 19. (The answers are under the Key vocabulary.)

Variation

Divide students into pairs and ask them all to look at Text A. When they have read it, stick several enlarged copies of Text B on the wall. In their pairs, students take turns to go and look at Text B and report any differences to their partner. They note the differences on their copy of Text A. The first pair to find and note down all the differences is the winner.

Follow-up

Write the following questions on the board:
How old were you when you started school? What do you remember about your first day at school? Who was your favourite teacher? What was your favourite lesson? Where did you sit, and who did you sit next to? Did you eat lunch at school or did you go home? What is your best and worst memory of that school?
Ask students to talk about these questions in pairs or small groups.

Homework

A Write some sentences about your first school, using the questions from the Follow-up.
B Find someone outside of the class and ask them the questions from the Follow-up. If necessary, ask them the questions in your first language. Then write down their answers in English.

Acknowledgement
The idea of 'the messenger and the scribe' comes from an activity of that name in *Dictation* by Paul Davis and Mario Rinvolucri (Cambridge University Press 1988).

Text A

I remember my first school very well. The headteacher was called Mr Jennings.

He was a strict man and everyone was very frightened of him. My classroom was on the first floor, at the end of a long corridor. It had thirty desks in rows, and I sat in the front row. There was a clock above the door. The clock was always slow, so we never knew what time it was.

We began the day with a reading lesson. Sometimes I forgot to bring my book to school, so I shared with my neighbour. We had a half-hour break at 10.30, and then we did art until lunchtime. I usually brought a packed lunch.

My favourite teacher was Mrs Rose. She came in the afternoons and taught us geography. She smiled a lot and her lessons were never boring. She showed us lots of maps and we sometimes listened to cassettes about interesting places. I loved my first school.

- ✂

Text B

I remember my first school very well. The headteacher was called Mr Jennings.

He was a kind man and everyone was very fond of him. My classroom was on the ground floor, at the end of a long corridor. It had twenty desks in rows, and I sat in the back row. There was a clock above the board. The clock was always fast, so we never knew what time it was.

We began the day with a writing lesson. Sometimes I forgot to bring my pencils to school, so I shared with my neighbour. We had a fifteen-minute break at 11 o'clock, and then we did music until lunchtime. I usually had lunch in the school canteen.

My favourite teacher was Mrs Rose. She came in the afternoons and taught us history. She laughed a lot and her lessons were never difficult. She showed us lots of pictures and we sometimes watched videos about interesting people. I loved my first school.

13.2

Secondary school: the best days of your life?

Level

Intermediate

Time

40–45 minutes

Aim

To aid recognition of vocabulary items related to experiences at secondary school, and provide speaking practice

Materials

One copy of the sheet for each group of three to four students

One dice for each group of three to four students

One counter (or equivalent) for each student

Key vocabulary

break time
classmate
detention
headteacher
school bully
teacher's pet
timetable
to be picked for the school team
to break up for the holidays
to get a place at university
to play truant
to return your library books
to win a school prize

School subjects
e.g. *Art, Language lessons, Music, PE, Science*

Verbs relating to exams
e.g. *do badly in, do well in, fail, pass, revise for, take*

Warm-up

1 Write the heading *Secondary school* on the board. Check that students understand which school years belong to the secondary level of education. Do a quick brainstorm of topic-related vocabulary.
2 Write on the board any of the words from the Key vocabulary that the students did not suggest in the brainstorm. Ask students to define them.

Main activity

1 Divide students into groups of three to four.
2 Give each group a copy of the sheet, a dice and a set of counters.
3 Playing the game:
   › Students place their counters on the start square and throw the dice. The student with the highest score begins.
   › Students take turns to throw the dice and move their counters along the board.
   › If the student lands on a topic square, e.g. school dinners, science lessons, they have to speak for one minute about that topic. Other members of the group are allowed to ask the student questions during this time.
   › If the student lands on another square, they should follow the instructions.
   › The first student to reach the finish is the winner.

Variation

If students land on a topic square, they nominate someone else in the group to talk on that topic. They may not nominate the student who was the last person to speak.

Follow-up

Students take turns to tell the rest of the class something that they learnt during the activity about another member of their group.

Homework

A Write 100 –150 words about *My best (or worst) experience at school*.
B Write 100 –150 words about *A teacher who influenced me a lot*.

35 My greatest achievement at school	**34** School dinners	**21** PE lessons	**20** You forgot to return your library books. Miss a turn.	**7** My best school friend	**6** The school year
36 You have got a place at university. Move on 3 spaces.	**33** You get a detention for being rude. Wait here until you throw a 6.	**22** You rescued a classmate from the school bully. Move on 2 spaces.	**19** My journey to school	**8** You were late for school today. Go back 2 spaces.	**5** You have passed all your exams. Move on 3 spaces.
37 A school trip I remember	**32** What I did at break times	**23** You didn't revise for a class test. Miss a turn.	**18** A typical daily timetable	**9** You have a piano lesson. Miss a turn.	**4** A lesson I hated
38 You did the wrong homework. Miss a turn.	**31** You worked in the school library instead of going to class. Go back 2 spaces.	**24** A lesson I loved	**17** A teacher I would like to forget	**10** Science lessons	**3** You left your school bag on the bus. Go back 2 spaces.
39 Your exam results are excellent. Have another turn.	**30** School has broken up for the holidays. Have another turn.	**25** Language lessons	**16** You helped a classmate with their homework. Move on 2 spaces.	**11** You have been picked for the school football team. Move on 2 spaces.	**2** You haven't finished your homework. Miss a turn.
Finish	**29** The headteacher	**26** You have failed all your exams. Go back 3 spaces.	**15** Art lessons	**12** You are the teacher's pet. Have another turn.	**1** A teacher I will always remember
40 You have missed the bus home. You cannot finish until you throw a 6.	**28** You have won first prize in the school poetry competition. Move on 2 spaces.	**27** A day when I missed school	**14** You get a detention for playing truant. Wait here until you throw a 6.	**13** Music lessons	**Start**

13.3

Successful learning

Level

Upper-intermediate
to advanced

Time

40–45 minutes

Aim

To practise vocabulary to
describe personal learning
styles

Materials

One copy of the sheet for each
student

One sheet of paper for each
group of three to four students

Key vocabulary

See photocopiable page
opposite

Warm-up

1   Divide students into pairs. Ask students to think of something that they learnt successfully, e.g. a
    new language or a computer programme, and of something else that they tried to learn, but with
    less success. Give pairs a few minutes to tell their stories to their partner.
2   Ask pairs to feedback to the whole class and write up any key vocabulary on the board.

Main activity

1   Give each student a copy of the sheet. Check that they understand all the vocabulary.
2   Ask them to complete the sheet individually. Encourage them to add their own ideas in the blank
    spaces in each list. Give them a time limit for this.
3   Divide the class into groups of three to four students. In their groups, students compare and
    discuss their answers, giving reasons for their choices.
4   After an appropriate time, tell the groups to write a list of five pieces of key advice for
    successful study.

Variation

After completing the sheets individually, students interview one another about how they completed
their sheet. After they have interviewed as many people as possible, students decide who they would
study most successfully with.

Follow-up

1   Display the lists around the classroom and divide the students into pairs. Ask the pairs to circulate
    around the classroom and read each list.
2   Pairs then vote on which list was the best and explain why.

Homework

A   Write 200–250 words on *How I learn best*, using vocabulary from the activity.
B   Write 200–250 words explaining the choices you made and what they reveal about your personality.

How do you learn best?

Tick a maximum of three options to complete each of the sentences.
If you don't agree with the options provided, you can write your own.

1 The kinds of classmates I like are ...

- ☐ supportive
- ☐ creative
- ☐ fun to be with
- ☐ truthful
- ☐ opinionated
- ☐ serious-minded
- ☐ similar to me
- ☐ different from me

----

2 The kind of teacher I prefer is ...

- ☐ authoritarian
- ☐ easy-going
- ☐ well-dressed
- ☐ knowledgeable
- ☐ caring
- ☐ unpredictable
- ☐ well-organised
- ☐ fair

----

3 My preferred place of learning ...

- ☐ is spacious
- ☐ has flexible seating
- ☐ has a carpeted floor
- ☐ has natural light
- ☐ has state-of-the-art equipment
- ☐ has a cosy atmosphere
- ☐ has a good view
- ☐ is very simply furnished and decorated

----

4 The strategies that help me most in my learning are ...

- ☐ time management
- ☐ reviewing my learning regularly
- ☐ writing detailed notes
- ☐ setting myself objectives and deadlines
- ☐ collaborating with other learners
- ☐ using a variety of materials and technical resources
- ☐ listening to relaxing music
- ☐ taking regular breaks

----

5 Sometimes during classroom lessons ...

- ☐ I switch off and lose my place
- ☐ I get uncomfortable and start to fidget
- ☐ I get distracted by other people
- ☐ I suddenly understand something that I'd been puzzling over for ages
- ☐ I wish the lesson didn't have to finish so soon
- ☐ I prefer to listen to the teacher than contribute myself
- ☐ my mind goes blank when I'm asked a question

----

6 When I work in a group I ...

- ☐ learn a lot from others
- ☐ have more fun
- ☐ like having a task in common
- ☐ feel more motivated
- ☐ get distracted from the learning task
- ☐ get impatient with people
- ☐ rely on other people
- ☐ dominate the group

14.1

Who, where and what?

Level

Elementary

Time

30–35 minutes

Aim

To practise basic job and workplace vocabulary

Materials

One set of pictures, cut up and put in an envelope, for each pair of students

For Variation, one set of pictures, cut up, for each student

For Variation, approximately 20 counters (or equivalent) for each student

For Homework B, one copy of the sheet, not cut up, for each student

Key vocabulary

cashier, supermarket, till
dentist, dental surgery, drill
farmer, field, tractor
hairdresser, hair salon, scissors
nurse, hospital, thermometer
police officer, police station, walkie-talkie
receptionist, hotel, computer
teacher, classroom, board
shop assistant, shop, clothes hanger
waiter, restaurant, plates

Warm-up

1 Draw on the board or show students a picture of someone doing an easily identifiable job, e.g. a cook or a firefighter. Ask students to identify the job.

2 Ask students *Where does he/she work?* (kitchen or restaurant for the cook; fire station for the firefighter). Ask students *What does he/she use?* (food, knives, saucepans, etc. for the cook; fire engine, ladder, etc. for the firefighter).

3 Teach any words from the Key vocabulary that will be new to your class by miming or drawing them.

Main activity

1 Divide students into pairs and ask the pairs to draw three columns with the headings *Who, Where, What*.

2 Give each pair an envelope containing the cut-up pictures. Ask students to sort the pictures into ten sets of three: Who (the worker); Where (where they work); What (what they use).

3 When the pairs have sorted all the cards into sets of three, ask them to write the words down in the appropriate columns, e.g. nurse, hospital, thermometer. Monitor and help as necessary.

4 When all the pairs have finished, check through the words and give pairs a mark for each picture correctly named and categorised.

Variation

This may also be used as a Follow-up after doing the Main activity.
Use the cards to play Bingo.

1 Give a set of cards and approximately 20 counters to each student. The counters may be coins or small pieces of paper. Tell each student to take 25 pictures from the envelope and arrange them face up in five rows of five.

2 Call out the words from the Key vocabulary in random order. If you call out a word for a picture that a student has in front of them, they may put a counter on that card.

3 The first student to complete a vertical, diagonal or horizontal row of counters shouts 'Bingo' and is the winner.

Follow-up

Place an envelope of pictures at the front of the classroom. Students take turns to pick a picture from the envelope and the rest of the class have to identify what they have chosen by asking yes/no questions, e.g. *Is it a job? Do you work outdoors? Do you use a computer?*, etc. With stronger classes you can tell students to think of other jobs which are not on the cards.

Homework

A Write a paragraph about your family or friends describing what jobs they do and where they work, e.g. *My mother is a dentist. She works in a dental surgery in the town centre. My father is an engineer. He works in a factory.*

B Write sentences using all the words illustrated on the sheet and add one more item which each person might use in their job, e.g. *A nurse works in a hospital. She uses a thermometer and a watch.*

14.2

Guess my job

Level

Intermediate

Time

35–40 minutes

Aim

To practise the language of jobs and their characteristics

Materials

One copy of the sheet, cut up and put in an envelope

For Variation, sticky tape

For Follow-up and Homework B, one copy of the sheet, not cut up, for each student

Key vocabulary

See photocopiable page opposite

Warm-up

1 Tell the class that you have a secret second job which they have to guess by asking you yes/no questions. Choose one of the jobs from the photocopiable page.

2 Brainstorm the kind of questions they might ask, e.g. *Do you work outdoors? Is it manual work? Are you well-paid? Do you need a degree or qualification to do this job?*

3 Students try to guess your job by asking yes/no questions. Put a mark on the board for each question that you answer. When students have guessed the job, count up the marks on the board. These are your total points.

Note: With weaker classes you may want to pre-teach some of the Key vocabulary they will not know.

Main activity

1 Place the envelope of cards at the front of the classroom. Ask a student to come and pick a card from the envelope and memorise what is on it. If they are unsure about the job chosen, they may check with you or a dictionary but should make sure that other students do not see or hear what the job is.

2 The other students then ask yes/no questions to determine what that student's job is.

3 Tell the student with the job card to keep a note of the number of questions asked. They win one point for each question asked.

4 The person who eventually guesses the job gets three points and is next to pick a card. If one student guesses further jobs correctly, that student gets three points again but nominates a different student to choose a card next.

5 Continue the game for an appropriate time or until all the cards have been used.

Variation

This may also be used as a Follow-up after doing the Main activity.

1 Give each student a job card and a piece of sticky tape. Tell them to stick their card on another student's back and make sure that the student does not know what the card is.

2 Students then move around the classroom asking each other yes/no questions in order to discover their job. The student they ask the question to looks at the card on their back and gives the appropriate answer. Encourage them to ask different questions to as many different students as possible.

3 The game continues until all the students have identified their jobs.

Follow-up

Give each student a copy of the sheet, not cut-up. Ask them to mark the five jobs they would most like to do with a tick and the five jobs they would least like to do with a cross. They then compare what they marked with two or three other students and explain why they would or would not like to do the jobs they marked. If there is time, check with the whole class which were the most and least popular jobs.

Homework

A Choose any job from the activity and write a paragraph about why you would or would not like to do that job.

B Divide your page into three columns with the following headings: *Job, Good points, Bad points.* Choose ten jobs from the photocopiable sheet and write them down in the first column. Then write down one good point and one bad point for each job you chose, e.g.
accountant / earn a lot of money / work can be boring

ballet dancer	travel agent	cook	accountant	builder	architect
lawyer	physicist	gardener	conductor (of an orchestra)	pop singer	politician
interpreter	surgeon	car mechanic	magician	English language teacher	airline pilot
weather forecaster	investment banker	vet	carpenter	baker	butcher
astronomer	chat show host	estate agent	model	journalist	plumber
painter and decorator	king or queen	lorry driver	clown	removal man	prison warder
poet	sculptor	fortune-teller	tour guide	web designer	computer programmer
dress designer	film critic	stunt person	anaesthetist	ski instructor	pizza delivery person

14.3 Dangerous and stressful jobs

Level

Upper-intermediate
to advanced

Time

40–45 minutes

Aim

To practise language of jobs
and talking about jobs

Materials

One set of cards, cut up, for
each group of three to four
students

Dictionaries may be useful

Key vocabulary

See photocopiable page
opposite

Warm-up

1 Ask students to write down (a) the most dangerous job they can think of, and (b) the most stressful job they can think of.

2 Divide the students into groups of three to four and ask them to compare the jobs they suggested. Ask them to decide what makes a job particularly dangerous or stressful.

Main activity

1 Give each group of three to four students a set of cards.

2 Explain that they have pictures of 24 jobs relating to a survey about the most dangerous and stressful jobs in the USA. The pictures can be divided into three categories; there is one picture that belongs to both of the first two categories.
    ▶ nine jobs that US insurance companies list as the most dangerous
    ▶ nine jobs that US insurance companies list as the most stressful
    ▶ seven jobs that are on neither the most dangerous nor the most stressful list

3 Tell students that they have about ten minutes to divide their cards into the three categories. Encourage the groups to discuss the reasons for their choices.

4 After ten minutes write the answers on the board and give each group a mark for each job which they put in the correct category.

Answers

Dangerous jobs – *firefighter, crew members of aircraft/boats/trains, tunneller, oil or gas rig worker, demolition contractor, steeplejack, miner, diver, asbestos worker*

Stressful jobs – *air traffic controller, astronaut, firefighter, mayor, National Football League player, osteopath, police officer, racing car driver, surgeon*

Neither list – *judge, acrobat, ambassador, army general, childminder, lifeguard, lumberjack*

Both lists – *firefighter*

5 Ask groups to rank each of the jobs in the two categories dangerous jobs and stressful jobs in order one to nine, beginning at one with the most dangerous or most stressful job.

6 Check and discuss answers with the whole class. Tell students to award themselves one point for every job they put in the correct position. The team with the highest score wins.

Answers

Most dangerous

1	asbestos worker	5	firefighter
2	crew members of aircraft/boats/trains	6	miner
		7	oil or gas rig worker
3	demolition contractor	8	steeplejack
4	diver	9	tunneller

Most stressful

1	firefighter	6	police officer
2	racing car driver	7	osteopath
3	astronaut	8	air traffic controller
4	surgeon		
5	National Football League player	9	mayor

Variation

Instead of doing step 5 in the Main activity, ask groups to note down at least one reason why each job is particularly dangerous or stressful. Give groups one point for each good reason suggested. They may not give the same reason for more than one job.

Follow-up

Ask students to discuss the jobs that were on neither list and consider how dangerous or stressful each could be. Then, if appropriate, ask them to discuss how dangerous or stressful they consider their job or the jobs of their friends and relatives to be.

Homework

A Write a paragraph about one job from the dangerous category and one from the stressful category explaining why they are dangerous or stressful.

B Write a job advert for one of the jobs from the activity. The advert should indicate what kind of qualifications, experience and qualities the job applicants should have.

acrobat	air traffic controller	ambassador	army general
asbestos worker	astronaut	childminder	crew members of aircraft/boats/trains
demolition contractor	diver	firefighter	judge
lifeguard	lumberjack	mayor	miner
National Football League player	oil or gas rig worker	osteopath	police officer
racing car driver	steeplejack	surgeon	tunneller

15.1

Bring and buy sale

Level

Elementary

Time

40–45 minutes

Aim

To practise talking about things you want to buy and sell, and what things cost

Materials

For Warm-up, one set of picture cards, cut up, for each pair of students

One *You'd like to buy…* card for each student

Enough cut-up picture cards to allow each student to have four pictures. Make sure that there are approximately the same number of copies of each picture.

Key vocabulary

afford, buy, cheap, expensive, good quality, sell, worth

alarm clock
bicycle
bookcase
briefcase
calculator
camera
CD player
chess set
guitar
lamp
mobile (phone)
personal stereo
rucksack
suitcase
surfboard
tennis racket

numbers and prices

Warm-up

1 Divide students into pairs and give each pair a set of cut-up picture cards. Check that they know the words for each of the items and write the words on the board.
2 Pretend that you want to buy an item from a student in the class. Ask them how much it is, but then try to buy it for a much cheaper price.
3 Write up the following key sentences on the board:
I want something cheaper.
It's not worth €10.
I'll give you €5 for it.
It's worth much more than that.
I'll take it.
It's a deal.
It's not what I'm looking for.
It's too expensive – I can't afford it.
It's very good quality.
Ask students to identify who would be more likely to use each sentence – the buyer or the seller. Collect the picture cards.

Main activity

1 Explain the idea of a bring and buy sale: this is a sale where everyone brings something to sell as well as looking for things to buy. Give each student one You'd like to buy card and four picture cards. If you have given a student a picture card which is one of the items on their You'd like to buy card, swap the picture for a different picture card.
2 Playing the game:
  ‣ Tell students that their aim is to sell as many of their objects as possible to other students and buy as many of the things on their list for the best price. Explain that all the items are second-hand and though some are older than others, they are all worth approximately the same.
  ‣ Tell students that they each have €50 to spend, but that they may also spend any money they receive from selling items.
  ‣ Give students about 15 minutes to move around the classroom trying to buy and sell their items. Encourage students to talk to as many people as possible in order to get the best price.
  ‣ If a student buys an item, they take that picture of the item. Students should keep a note of how much they spend and receive for each item they sell.
  ‣ After you have stopped the activity, tell students to count up their scores. Allow students two points for every item that has been sold and two points for every item that has been bought. Also allow students one extra point for every €5 they still have (e.g. if they still have €50 they would have 10 extra points).

Variation

Students work in pairs and first have to agree on what prices they want to sell or buy things for.

Follow-up

Students tell the rest of the class: what they bought and at what price; what they sold and at what price; how much money they have left.
As a whole class decide which student did best in the bring and buy sale.

Homework

A Write a list of ten things you bought recently. Beside each item write in words how much it cost.
B What countries have you visited or do you know about? What is cheap and what is expensive there, compared to your own country? Write a short paragraph.

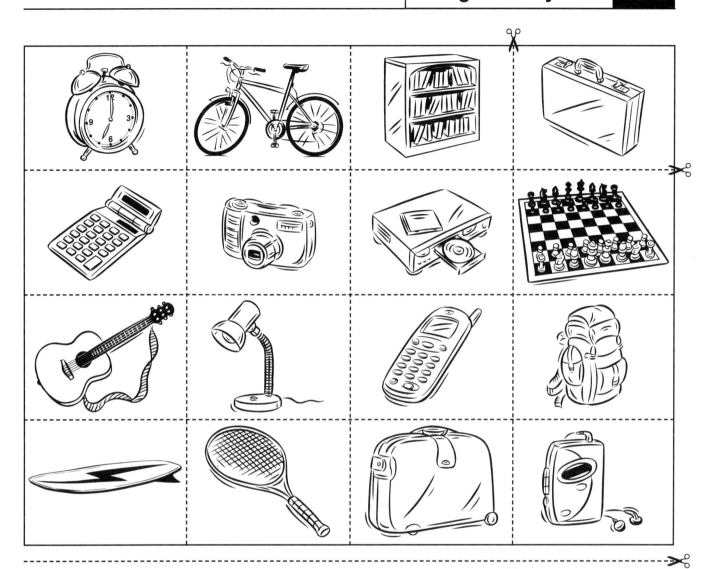

You'd like to buy a bicycle, a **CD** player and a chess set.	You'd like to buy a camera, a guitar and a briefcase.	You'd like to buy a suitcase, a tennis racket and a **CD** player.	You'd like to buy an alarm clock, a bookcase and a camera.
You'd like to buy a **CD** player, a personal stereo and a lamp.	You'd like to buy a guitar, a rucksack and a surfboard.	You'd like to buy a tennis racket, a surfboard and a bicycle.	You'd like to buy a bookcase, a lamp and a rucksack.
You'd like to buy a personal stereo, a mobile phone and a bookcase.	You'd like to buy a rucksack, a calculator and a tennis racket.	You'd like to buy a surfboard, a briefcase and a mobile phone.	You'd like to buy a table lamp, a chess set and a calculator.
You'd like to buy a mobile phone, a camera and an alarm clock.	You'd like to buy a calculator, a suitcase and a bicycle.	You'd like to buy a briefcase, an alarm clock and a guitar.	You'd like to buy a chess set, a suitcase and a personal stereo.

15.2 Crossword conversations

Level

Intermediate

Time

40–45 minutes

Aim

To practise recognising vocabulary used in dialogues about money and shopping, and defining words

Materials

For Warm-up, one set of dialogue cards, cut up and put in an envelope, for each pair of students

One copy of Crosswords A and B for each pair of students

Key vocabulary

bargain
bill
browse
cash
change
counter
credit card
discount
fare
fitting room
invest
overcharge
overdrawn
pension
receipt
refund
savings account
special offer
subscription
till
worth

Warm up

1   Divide the class into pairs and give each pair an envelope containing a set of dialogue strips.
2   Ask students to match the first part of each dialogue with the second part. Then check answers with the class.
3   Then ask students to identify all the items of vocabulary in the dialogues relating to money and shopping. Explain any new words and check that students understand the meanings. Then collect the dialogue strips.
●   Variation on Warm-up:
For a more challenging Warm-up give each pair a sheet showing only the second half of each dialogue. Ask students to write a suitable first half for each one.

Main activity

1   In their pairs give one student a copy of Crossword A and give the other student a copy of Crossword B. They should not look at each other's crosswords.
2   Explain that both crosswords have vocabulary from the earlier activity. On Crossword A all the down words are missing, and on Crossword B all the across words are missing.
3   Tell the students that their task is to give each other clues for each of the missing words on their partner's crossword. Students take turns to say a number and ask their partner for a clue.
4   When students have completed their crosswords, they may check their answers with one another.
5   If students finish early, ask them to try to remember the original dialogues where each word appeared.

Variations

1   Divide the class into two halves. Give copies of Crossword A to one half of the class, and give copies of Crossword B to the other half.
2   The students work with a partner from their own half of the class and together they write clues for the words in their crossword. Both students need to write down the set of clues.
3   Students then exchange their set of clues with a student from the other half of the class. Then, individually, they try to complete the crossword using the clues they received.

Follow-up

Choose a word from the crossword and make students ask you yes/no questions to try and work out which word you are thinking of, e.g. *Is it a word for a sum of money? Is it a noun? Is it a piece of paper?* After demonstrating the activity, students take it in turns to do the same in pairs.

Homework

A   Write a dialogue that might take place in a shop using some of the language practised in the activity.
B   Write a set of clues for the 18 words in the crossword.

Can I have my money back please?	I'm sorry, we don't give refunds.
Why aren't you travelling by train?	I can't afford the fare.
Were those shoes expensive?	Not at all. They were a real bargain.
Are you going to buy that new coat?	I can't. My account is already overdrawn.
Do you want to pay by credit card?	No, I'll pay cash.
When is your father retiring?	Next year. He's looking forward to getting his pension!
I can't possibly eat any more.	Neither can I. Let's ask for the bill.
Have you got anything smaller than a €20 note?	I'm sorry, I've run out of change.
I'd like to open a savings account.	Certainly. How much do you want to invest?
I'm afraid I've broken your vase.	Don't worry. It wasn't worth anything.
I think I've been overcharged.	Really? Could you show me your receipt please?
Where do I pay for these?	There's a till over there, near the door.
I paid €4 for this shampoo last week. Now it's only €3.50.	It's on special offer.
Do you get this magazine by post every month?	Yes, I pay an annual subscription.
How many tickets would you like?	Ten please. Do we get a group discount?
Can I try this jacket on before I buy it?	Of course. I'll show you to our fitting room.
Are you looking for anything in particular?	Not really. I'm just browsing.
Do you sell fresh prawns?	Yes we do. They're over on the fish counter.

A

B

15.3

Get rich quick quiz

Level

Upper-intermediate to advanced

Time

35–45 minutes

Aim

To introduce and review words and phrases related to money, buying and selling

Materials

For Follow-up and Homework B, one copy of the sheet for each student

Key vocabulary

Note: These words should not be actively taught as it will ruin the fun of guessing.

allowance
be in the black
be in the red
benefit
be well off
come into money
currency
denomination
exchange rate
golden handshake
guarantee
inheritance
joint account
live from hand to mouth
mortgage
pension
rainy day
rebate
receipt
round (of drinks)
spend money like water
subsidy
tighten your belt
treat
windfall

Warm-up

1 Ask students what they would do with a million Euros, or the equivalent in your currency, if they won it in a competition.

2 Tell students that they are going to have the opportunity to win up to a million Euros by taking part in a quiz, and all the questions are about the language of money.

Main activity

1 Divide students into teams of two or three students. Each team should choose a name for itself. Write the names of the teams on the board and draw a column under each name.

2 Explain that there are 15 multiple-choice questions each worth a certain amount of money. For each correct answer they win money and the amount they can win gradually increases.

3 Tell students the value of the first question, then read aloud the question and the four possible answers. Give the teams 20 seconds to choose the right answer and write it down.

4 Continue in the same way until you have asked all the questions.

5 Ask a representative from each team to come up to the board with their answers. Then check the answers with the whole class. The team representatives fill in the columns on the board with the amounts of money won for each correct answer.

6 The winners are the team with the most money.

Answers

1a 2d 3c 4b 5b 6b 7c 8c 9a 10a 11b 12d 13a 14b 15a

Follow-up

1 Give each student a copy of the sheet and ask them to circle the correct answers. Then ask students to underline any alternative answers which are real English.

2 As a class, discuss the meanings of these alternative answers.

Homework

A Prepare another set of 15 questions like this quiz but on another topic such as economics and business. Bring your quiz for other students to do in the next lesson.

B Look at the 15 correct answers to the questions on the sheet. Write sentences of your own to illustrate how these words or expressions are used.

	WIN
1 If your bank account is overdrawn, are you: (a) in the red? (b) in the pink? (c) in the orange? (d) in the black?	€40,000
2 You buy a hairdryer but it doesn't work. You take it back to the shop. Do you ask for: (a) a receipt? (b) a guarantee? (c) a rebate? (d) a refund?	€45,000
3 The Japanese yen, the American dollar, the Brazilian real, and the Indian rupee are all examples of different: (a) denominations (b) coins (c) currencies (d) exchange rates	€55,000
4 What is a mortgage? (a) inherited money or land (b) a loan to buy a house or flat (c) an initial payment to guarantee a later purchase (d) subsidy to help students pay for tuition	€60,000
5 Your friend invites you out for a meal and insists on paying. He or she says: (a) This is my gift. (b) This is my treat. (c) This is my offer. (d) This is my round.	€60,000
6 When two people, e.g. a husband and wife, share the same bank account it is called: (a) a sharing account (b) a joint account (c) a deposit account (d) a partnership account	€60,000
7 In many countries when you are too old to work, the government pays you: (a) an inheritance (b) an allowance (c) a pension (d) a benefit	€65,000
8 When someone retires from work after a long period of service, they may be given a golden: (a) goodbye (b) gesture (c) handshake (d) wave	€65,000
9 If you receive some money unexpectedly, you may call it: (a) a windfall (b) a rainfall (c) a waterfall (d) a snowfall	€65,000
10 If a rich member of your family dies, it is possible that you will: (a) come into some money (b) fall into some money (c) move into some money (d) get into some money	€75,000
11 If a person spends money carelessly, we say that they are spending money: (a) like juice (b) like water (c) like rain (d) like chocolate	€75,000
12 Your expenses have increased but your salary has not. Should you: (a) tighten your purse? (b) tighten your trousers? (c) tighten your collar? (d) tighten your belt?	€75,000
13 If you have hardly enough money to live on, you are said to be living: (a) from hand to mouth (b) from moment to moment (c) from eye to stomach (d) from day to day	€80,000
14 Another way of saying that a person is very rich is to say that they are: (a) well in (b) well off (c) well over (d) well up	€80,000
15 If you save money for the future, you may say you are putting it by for: (a) a rainy day (b) a black day (c) a red-letter day (d) a bad hair day	€100,000

16.1

Past time dominoes

Level

Elementary

Time

35–40 minutes

Aim

To practise using words and prepositions in past time expressions

Materials

One set of dominoes, cut up, for each group of three students

Key vocabulary

in + months
in January, in February, etc.

in + seasons
in spring, in summer, etc.

on + days
on Sunday, on Wednesday, on 6 January, on my birthday, on Christmas Day, on New Year's Day, etc.

at + times of day
at midday, at midnight, at 7 o'clock, etc.

for + periods of time
for a week, for a long time, for six months, for ten years, etc.

last + days, weeks, months, years
last night, last weekend, last year

periods of time + ago
six months ago, ten years ago, etc.

yesterday, last night, last weekend, last month, last year

Warm-up

1 Draw seven columns on the board. Label the columns: *in, on, at, for, last, ago* and put a dash (–) to represent 'no word' in the last column.

2 Ask the students to form a queue in front of the board. Choose a word from the Key vocabulary, e.g. *February*, and write it in the correct column, i.e. the *in* column. Now give the first student a pen. Say another word from the Key vocabulary, e.g. *Christmas Day*, and ask the student to write it in the correct column.

3 Check each answer with the class. Continue in this way until each student has had a go. If students prefer to stay in their seats, let them tell you which column to write the words in.

Main activity

1 Draw a few four-sided dominoes from the sheet on the board. Ask students how they can be fitted together to form the right connections.

2 Divide the students into groups of three. Give each group a set of dominoes. Tell each person to take five dominoes and to place the rest face down in a pile.

3 Playing the game:
   ‣ Student A starts by placing one domino on the table.
   ‣ Student B places a domino beside the first one so that the two adjoining words make a time expression. The group should decide if it is correct or not.
   ‣ Student C places a third domino beside the second one. The line can go in any direction but each domino must be placed next to the last one put down. So for example, Student C's domino may not be placed next to Student A's domino.
   ‣ If a student cannot place a domino, they take one from the pile and wait until it is their turn again.
   ‣ The winner is the first person to put down all their dominoes.

Variation

Divide students into pairs and give each pair a set of dominoes. Together students try to create a line in which all the dominoes are used. The first pair to complete a correctly connected line wins.

Follow-up

In their groups or as a whole class, students make up their own sentences about the past, using the time expressions from the game. They get one point for each correct sentence.

Homework

A Ask students to write six sentences about themselves, using the past time expressions they have practised.

B Ask students to prepare six questions with some past time expressions to use to interview a classmate or another person, e.g. *What did you do last weekend? When did you last go on holiday?* This kind of interview can also be done on email.

Acknowledgement
We have adapted the idea of four-sided dominoes from *Pronunciation Games* by Mark Hancock (Cambridge University Press 1995).

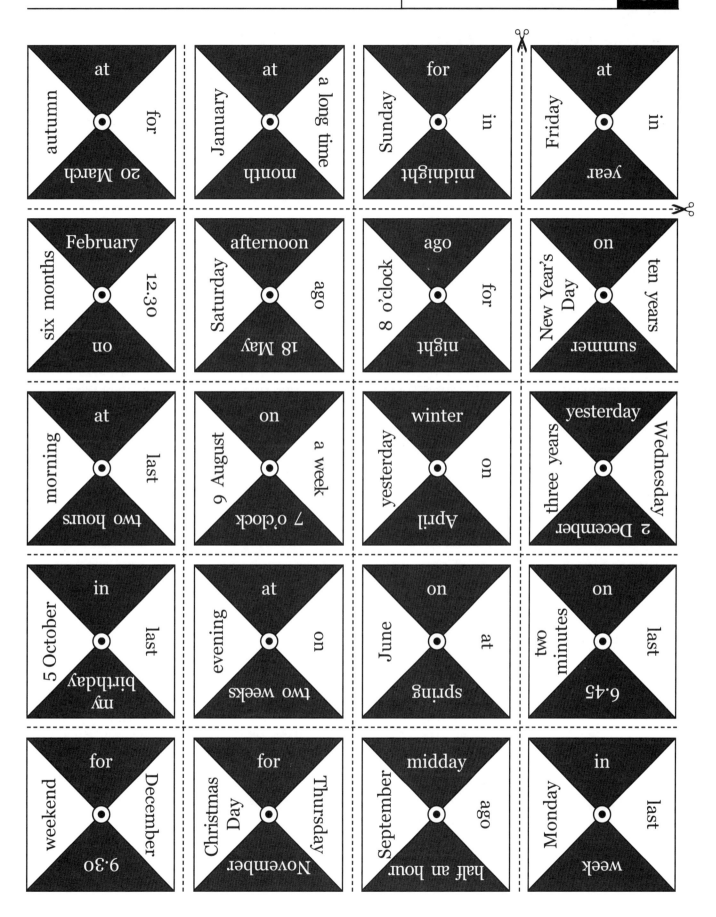

16.2

Phrasal verbs auction

Level

Intermediate

Time

40–45 minutes

Aim

To focus students' attention on the meaning and use of some common phrasal verbs

Materials

For Warm-up, one set of Phrasal verb cards, cut up, for each pair of students

One set of Sentences for auction for each pair of students

Key vocabulary

break down
break up
bring up
cut down on
cut off
cut out
find out
give up
let down
put across
put down
put through
run out of
take after
take on
take up
tell off

Warm-up

1 Elicit some phrasal verbs that students are already familiar with by miming or paraphrasing, e.g. *put your coat on, turn the light off, the plane took off at 10.30.*

2 Divide students into pairs. Give each pair a set of Phrasal verb cards. Tell them to spread them out on the table and find the matching pairs, i.e. sentence and correct particle(s).

3 When everyone has finished, check that they have the correct pairs and ask students to explain the meaning of each phrasal verb. Then collect in the cards before starting the Main activity.

Main activity

1 Explain what happens at an auction and introduce some of the associated vocabulary, e.g. *auctioneer, hammer, to bid for something, going, going, gone!, sold!.*

2 Tell the students they have €5000, or the equivalent in their currency, to spend at the auction. The lowest acceptable bid is €200. Their aim is to buy as many correct sentences as possible.

3 First ask pairs to decide on their maximum bid for each sentence, and write it in the first column. Resist giving any clues about whether sentences are correct or not.

4 To begin the auction read out the sentences one at a time and ask for bids. Sell each sentence to the highest bidders and tell them to write down in the second column of the auction sheet how much they paid.

5 When all the sentences have been auctioned, go through the list and tell students whether each sentence was correct or not. Try not to elicit the correct sentences until the Follow-up.

6 The winners are the students who have bought the most correct sentences.

Answers

The incorrect sentences are – 3 (broke down), 4 (took me on), 8 (let me down), 9 (give up), 11 (put me through to).

Variation

Ask a student to take on the role of auctioneer.

Follow-up

Ask students to change each incorrect sentence into a correct sentence. Check suggested corrections with the whole class.

Homework

A Look up each of the phrasal verbs from the activity in a monolingual English dictionary and note down more examples of their use.

B Write questions for a class survey in the following lesson, using phrasal verbs from the activity, e.g. *Where were you brought up? What would you most like to cut down on?*

Acknowledgement

As far as we know, the idea of auctioning language items was first suggested in *Grammar Games* by Mario Rinvolucri (Cambridge University Press 1984).

Phrasal verb cards

after	He took .... his mother in both looks and personality.	up	We had almost given .... hope that he was still alive.
on	She was taken .... as a laboratory assistant.	up	She decided to take .... medicine as a career.
down	She broke .... in tears when she failed her driving test again.	up	They broke .... just a month before their wedding.
through	I phoned reception and they put me .... to customer services.	off	Her father told her .... for coming home so late.
down	She was her father's least favourite child and he always put her	off	Six villages were cut .... by the heavy snow that had fallen overnight.
across	He found it hard to put his ideas .... to the other committee members.	down on	To save money she tried to cut .... her number of shopping trips.
up	After her husband left she brought .... their children on her own.	out	We phoned the cinema to find .... what time the movie started.
out of	They ran .... money so they had to find work to pay the bills.	down	He said he would finish the work by Friday but he let me ....

Sentences for auction

		Maximum bid	Price paid
1	My father always said I took after him but I don't agree.		
2	After my parents died I was brought up by my grandparents.		
3	When she heard the sad news she broke up and cried.		
4	The job interview went badly, so I was surprised when they took me up.		
5	The car ran out of petrol on the way home.		
6	At school I was always being told off for talking in class.		
7	Why did Bill and Judy break up?		
8	Jane really let me out by not helping me when I needed her so badly.		
9	I had to give in my job because I hated my boss.		
10	Even though she cut down on sweets, she was still very overweight.		
11	The receptionist put me across to Mr White's extension.		
12	Did you manage to find out what the film was about?		
13	My manager always used to put me down in front of other people.		
14	To help improve my concentration I took up yoga.		

16.3

What a great story!

Level

Upper-intermediate
to advanced

Time

40–45 minutes

Aim

To practise vocabulary for
talking about a film or book you
have enjoyed

Materials

One set of cards, cut up and put
in an envelope, for each group
of three to four students.

One copy of the Film summary
headings for each student

Dictionaries may be useful

Key vocabulary

See photocopiable page
opposite

Warm-up

1 Ask if any of the students have seen a film recently. What films have they seen? Did they enjoy them?
2 Write the following list of genres on the board: *animation, epic, historical adventure, melodrama, romantic comedy, satire, sci-fi, thriller, western*. Ask them for names of films which match these genres.
3 Ask students which of these they prefer and why. Give them a few minutes to discuss in pairs a film they have seen recently, or the type of film they most like or dislike.

Main activity

1 Divide the students into groups of three to four and make sure that each group has a dictionary.
2 Give a set of cut-up cards to each group. Tell them to discuss the words and categorise them into four groups under these headings: genre, storyline/plot, setting, characters. Tell students that they have these categories on cards in the set of cards you have given them. (A possible categorisation is indicated on the photocopiable sheet opposite, but answers may vary.)
3 Monitor and help as necessary. When students have finished discuss answers with the whole class.
4 Give each student a copy of the whole sheet. Check that they understand all the film summary headings.
5 Ask students to think of a film with a good story, and to write a three-paragraph summary of the film using the Film summary headings. They must not give the title of the film and should avoid directly naming the characters or the actors who play them.

Variation

This activity can also be used in the same way to write reviews of books.

Follow-up

Students exchange their film summaries with a partner and try to guess the name of the film, using the information and asking one another questions to get more details.

Homework

A Write the story of your partner's film based on your partner's film summary and the additional information you got from the questions you asked them.
B Write a review of a film you have enjoyed, using as many of the words from the activity as possible.

genre	animation	epic	historical adventure	melodrama
romantic comedy	satire	sci-fi	thriller	western
storyline/ plot	biographical	contrived	convoluted	disturbing
entertaining	episodic	gripping	moving	(un)predictable
sentimental	slow-moving	thought-provoking	thrilling	true-life
setting	bizarre	contemporary	everyday	fairytale
futuristic	historical	macabre	spectacular	surreal
characters	(un)believable	comic	(un)convincing	eccentric
endearing	engaging	exaggerated	heroic	menacing
monstrous	pretentious	tragic	villainous	mysterious

Film summary headings

Film genre	Opening sequence	Special highlights of the film
Setting	Main events	My opinion of the film (three
Main characters	Climax	adjectives)
Summary of plot (one sentence)	Closing sequence	

17.1

A day in the modern office

Level

Elementary

Time

40-45 minutes

Aim

To practise vocabulary relating to working in a modern office, particularly language relating to computer use

Materials

For Warm-up, one copy of picture A for each student

One copy of picture B for each pair of students

For Variation, one copy of picture A and one copy of picture B for each pair of students

Key vocabulary

calendar
CD
chair
coffee machine
cursor
desk
desktop computer
fax machine
floppy disk
hardware
icon
laptop
map
mouse
photocopier
print
printer
save
software
table
title of document

Warm-up

Give each student a copy of picture A. Ask them to describe and memorise the picture in as much detail as possible. Make sure that all the words in the Key vocabulary are used in the course of this activity. After the picture has been fully described, collect in all the pictures.

Main activity

1 Divide the students into pairs and give each pair a copy of picture B.
2 Pairs look at the pictures and try to find the 12 differences between picture B and the picture they looked at in the Warm-up. When they find a difference, tell students to note it down.
3 After about five minutes, stop the students and ask which differences they found. Which pair found most differences?
4 After students have given their answers, give each pair a copy of picture A and ask them to find any remaining differences.

Answers

Picture A	Picture B
Woman is moving mouse with left hand	*with right hand*
There is a floppy disk on her desk	*a CD on her desk*
The cursor is pointing to the 'print' icon	*to the 'save' icon*
The title of the document is 'Annual Report 2003'	*'Annual Report 2004'*
The company name is 'Software Solutions'	*'Hardware Solutions'*
The clock reads 12:15	*reads 12:20*
The window is slightly open	*is closed*
The map is of Great Britain	*is of the world*
The man's computer is a desktop computer	*is a laptop*
The coffee machine is on a desk	*is on a chair*
The fax machine is on the left of the printer	*is on the right of the printer*
There is a calendar above the photocopier	*there is no calendar above the photocopier*

Variation

Students do not look at one of the pictures as suggested in the Warm-up. Instead, they are divided into pairs, and each take one of the pictures. They may not look at each other's picture but should describe their own picture to their partner. They try to discover what the twelve differences are by listening carefully to each other's descriptions and asking further questions if they wish to.

Follow-up

Students work in pairs and write a description of the office in picture A. However, they should alter their description in at least five ways from the office in picture A (but in different ways from picture B). They give their description to another pair which must find where the five differences are.

Homework

A Write a description of a modern office that you know or the type of office that you would like to work in.
B If possible, look at a computer programme which you are familiar with and which has its commands in English. Look at the different menus and make a note of the different commands in each menu. What do each of them mean?

A

B

17.2

Sci-tech board game

Level

Intermediate

Time

35–45 minutes

Aim

To revise basic words for inventions and sciences

Materials

One copy of the sheet for each group of four to five students

One dice for each group of four to five students

One counter (or equivalent) for each student

For Follow-up, one small piece of paper for each student

Key vocabulary

explorer, invention, inventor

Sciences
e.g. *biology, botany, chemistry, genetics, meteorology, physics, zoology*

Scientists
e.g. *biologist, botanist, chemist, geneticist, meteorologist, physicist, zoologist*

Gadgets
e.g. *penknife, stapler, tin opener*

Inventions
e.g. *camera, computer, DVD player, fridge, mobile phone, satellite, telephone, TV, video recorder, washing machine*

Names of planets
e.g. *Mars, Jupiter, Saturn*

Types of transport
e.g. *bicycle, boat, bus, car, helicopter, motorbike, plane, ship, train*

Materials
e.g. *fabric, metal, plastic, wood*

Warm-up

Write the categories of Key vocabulary on the board, i.e. *Sciences, Scientists, Gadgets*, etc. Check that students understand the categories by asking them to give you a few examples of words in each category.

Main activity

1   Divide students into groups of four to five. Give each group a copy of the sheet and a dice. Each student also needs a counter.
2   Players take it in turns to throw the dice and move round the board from the start square. If they land on a square with words, they follow the instructions.
3   Players may not name something that has already been named in the game. One person in the group should note down each word that is named in the game.
4   If students are not sure if an answer is correct, they may check with the teacher. If a player cannot do what the instructions ask them to do, they miss a turn.
5   The winner is the first player to throw the number that takes them exactly to the finish square.
6   When groups have finished playing the game, ask them to count up the number of words named. The group that has the most words written down is the winning group.

Variation

Before playing the game, ask students to fill in the blank squares on the board with additional instructions of their own. They then play the game. After the game, groups tell each other what extra instructions they added and how well they worked.

Follow-up

This may be done as either a whole class activity or with groups of four to six students, depending on the size of the class.
1   Give each student a small piece of paper and ask them to write down:
      a   the name of a means of transport
      b   the name of a science
      c   the name of an invention
2   Tell students to pass their piece of paper to the person sitting on their right.
3   Students then take it in turns to define the three words they have been given for the other students in the group to guess. The person who wrote the words is obviously not allowed to guess. The student defining the words is not allowed to use those words in their definitions.

Homework

A   Describe three inventions which are very important to you. Write about 100 words to explain why these inventions are particularly important to you.
B   Write a list of sciences and their corresponding scientists, e.g. *physics – physicist*. Use a dictionary to help you.

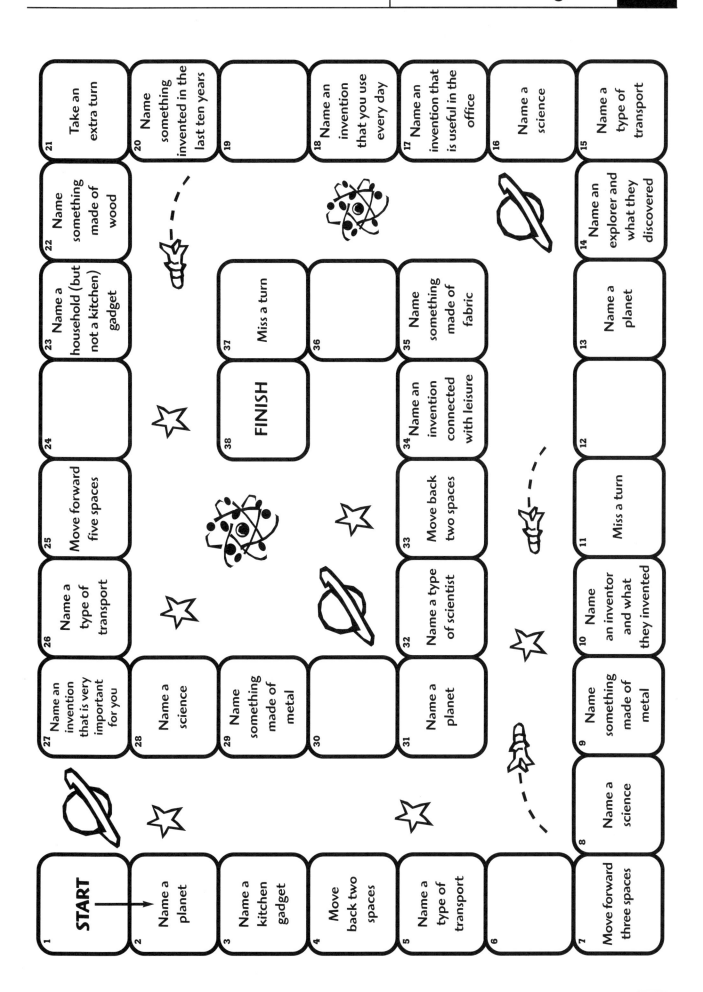

START

1

2 Name a planet

3 Name a kitchen gadget

4 Move back two spaces

5 Name a type of transport

6

7 Move forward three spaces

8 Name a science

9 Name something made of metal

10 Name an inventor and what they invented

11 Miss a turn

12

13 Name a planet

14 Name an explorer and what they discovered

15 Name a type of transport

16 Name a science

17 Name an invention that is useful in the office

18 Name an invention that you use every day

19

20 Name something invented in the last ten years

21 Take an extra turn

22 Name something made of wood

23 Name a household (but not a kitchen) gadget

24

25 Move forward five spaces

26 Name a type of transport

27 Name an invention that is very important for you

28 Name a science

29 Name something made of metal

30

31 Name a planet

32 Name a type of scientist

33 Move back two spaces

34 Name an invention connected with leisure

35 Name something made of fabric

36

37 Miss a turn

38 FINISH

17.3 Definitions

Level

Upper-intermediate
to advanced

Time

30–40 minutes

Aim

To review vocabulary relating
to various aspects of science
and technology and to practise
giving concise definitions

Materials

For Warm-up, one set of cards,
cut up and put in an envelope,
for each pair of students

For Warm-up, dictionaries may
be useful

Sets of cards, cut up and put in
an envelope, either just one set
for the whole class or enough
for each group of six to ten
students

For Homework B, one copy of
the sheet, not cut up, for each
student

Key vocabulary

See photocopiable sheet
opposite

Warm-up

1 Write the following five categories on the board: *computers*, *entertainment*, *transport*, *work*, *science*.

2 Divide students into pairs and give each pair an envelope of words. Tell students to divide the cards into the five categories and to check the meanings of any words they do not know. Monitor and help as necessary.

3 Check answers with the whole class. Note that some of the words may fit into more than one category, so students may have different answers. This is fine as long as students can justify their answers. Collect the envelopes of words.

Main activity

1 This activity may be done as either a whole class activity or in groups of six to ten students. The class or each group needs one envelope of words.

2 Each student takes turns to pick a word from the envelope. They have to define their word as quickly as possible for the other students in the class to guess, but they may not use any of the words on the card. For example, if they were defining *bicycle pump*, they may not use either *bicycle* or *pump* in their definition. If they do so, they lose a point and the game passes immediately to the next student whose turn it is to give a definition. The first person to guess what is being defined gets three points.

3 Play continues until each student has had at least one chance to define a word.

Variation

Play the game in pairs. Students take turns to pick a word from the envelope and define it for their partner to guess. Play continues until all the words have been guessed. The pair that defines and guesses all the words in the envelope first is the winner.

Follow-up

Students work in pairs taking it in turns to pick a word from their envelope and try to draw it for their partner to guess. Which pair can draw and guess most words in five minutes?

Homework

A Take one of the areas that these words focus on, i.e. *computing*, *transport*, *work*, *entertainment* or *science*, and write 100–200 words describing how you think this will be different in the future. Use some of the words from the activity.

B Write all the words from the sheet in one of these columns:

Useful for me directly   *Useful for me indirectly*   *Not useful for me in any way*

webcam	database	computer screen	computer virus	chatroom	email address
cybercafé	FAQs	search engine	modem	video conferencing	dubbing
subtitles	extension lead	DVD	cable TV	karaoke machine	autocue
sci-fi	satellite TV	digital TV	estate car	bicycle pump	handlebar
glove compartment	jack	gearbox	cockpit	fuselage	limo
black box	teleworking	voicemail	rat race	telesales	smart card
hotline	pager	battery	magnet	comet	test tube
planet	eclipse	microscope	genetic engineering	genetic fingerprinting	animal testing
euthanasia	clone	photo-sensitivity	magnifying glass	DNA	valve

18.1

Find five

Warm-up

1 Give each student a copy of the sheet. Check that students understand the categories and elicit one example for each category.
2 Tell students to write that example word in the first column on their sheet.

Main activity

1 Ask students to complete the rest of the sheet individually, finding at least four more examples for each catergory.
2 Stop the activity after an appropriate time.
3 Tell students to work with a partner and to compare how many words they each managed to think of.
4 Check answers with the whole class.

Variation

Students work in groups of three to four rather than individually and have to find as many words for each category as they can. Tell students they get one point for the first five words in each category and then two points for each word after that. Stop play after ten minutes and see which group has won the most points.

Follow-up

1 In pairs, students choose six words they found in the Main activity. They then jumble the letters of those words to create six anagrams.
2 Tell pairs to exchange their anagrams with another pair. Students try to unjumble the letters and then check their answers with the other pair.

Homework

A List all the new words you would like to learn from this activity and draw pictures to help you remember them. You may want to use a picture dictionary to help you.
B This is part of an email you receive from a new pen friend. Write your reply.

Tell me about your country. I am particularly interested in animals. What kind of wild animals are there in your country? What domestic animals do people have?
Also, what is the countryside like? Do you have mountains, good beaches, big lakes, forests or deserts? Please tell me all you can.
Eric

Category	1	2	3	4	5
Landscape features					
Wild animals					
Domestic animals					
Countries					
In the sky					
Things that grow					
Water features					

18.2

Social survey

Level

Intermediate

Time

30–35 minutes

Aim

To practise vocabulary relating to social issues like crime, government and the environment

Materials

One copy of the sheet for each student

For Homework B, an extra copy of the sheet for each student

Key vocabulary

armed forces
death penalty
disease
drought
earthquake
eco-friendly
education
facility
famine
fine
flood
forest fire
genetically modified food
global warming
government
health care
hurricane
mode of transport
murder
organic food
overpopulation
pollution
poverty
president
prime minister
prison
punishment
recycle
shoplifting
shortage of natural resources
snowstorm
unemployment
war

Warm-up

1 Ask students to suggest any social and environmental problems that they can think of. Try to elicit some of the words from the Key vocabulary.

2 Write on the board any of the words from the Key vocabulary that you think your students may not know. Elicit or explain what these words mean.

Main activity

1 Give each student a copy of the sheet. Ask them to complete the survey. Set students a time limit of approximately ten minutes.

2 When all students have completed their sheets, divide the class into groups of three to four students.

3 Ask students to discuss and explain their answers to their group.

Variation

Ask students to complete their sheets individually. Then allow students to move around the classroom interviewing as many other students as possible in order to find a partner with the most similar answers.

Follow-up

Discuss with the whole class the more open-ended questions from the survey or any questions that you feel your students will find particularly interesting or controversial.

Homework

A Choose three of the questions from the sheet and write a few sentences giving and explaining your opinion.

B Use the sheet to interview someone from outside the class and note down their answers in English.

Social issues survey

1 What do you think your government should spend most money on – education, health care or the armed forces?

....

2 Would you prefer to live in a big city, a small town or a village? Why?

....

3 What do you do to be eco-friendly, e.g. recycle paper/glass?

....

4 What do you think should be the punishment for murder – the death penalty, life in prison, or something else?

....

5 What do you think should be the punishment for shoplifting – prison, a fine, or something else?

....

6 What would be the first change you would make if you became Prime Minister or President of your country?

....

7 What new facility would you like to see in the town you live in at the moment?

....

8 Do you try to eat organic food and avoid genetically modified food? Why?

....

9 What is your favourite mode of transport? Why?

....

10 What transport-related problems have you experienced? What could be done to solve them?

....

11 Which three of these do you think are the main problems for the future of the world – poverty, famine, unemployment, war, disease, pollution, overpopulation, global warming, shortage of natural resources?

....

12 Which of these have you personally experienced – drought, flood, earthquake, hurricane, snowstorm, forest fire?

....

18.3 Compounds

Level

Upper-intermediate to advanced

Time

35–45 minutes

Aim

To practise common compound nouns related to the theme of social and environmental issues

Materials

For Warm-up and Main activity, one set of cards, cut up and put in an envelope, for each group of three to four students

For Homeworks A and B, one copy of the sheet for each student

Key vocabulary

acid rain
animal rights
battery farming
black market
blood sports
bottle bank
capital punishment
drug addiction
football hooligan
global warming
greenhouse effect
health hazard
litter bin
oil slick
ozone layer
power cut
road rage
sexual harassment
shanty town
sniffer dog
traffic jam
waste disposal
water shortage
welfare state

Note that although some other compounds are possible, e.g. blood bank, students will only be able to use all the cards if they make the compounds listed above

Warm-up

1   Check that students understand what compound nouns are. Elicit some examples, including one or two from the Key vocabulary list, if possible.
2   Divide students into groups of three to four. Give each group an envelope of word cards and ask them to match the cards to form compound nouns.
3   Check answers with the whole class and tell them to divide the compounds into groups in any appropriate way, e.g. compounds related to crime. Then ask students to explain their categorisation to other groups.

Main activity

1   In the same groups, students shuffle the cards and deal seven cards to each player. The rest are placed face down in a pile.
2   Playing the game:
   ▸   Students look at their cards and put any complete compound words to one side. Each student then places any one of their unpaired cards face up on the table.
   ▸   Players take turns to play.
       Either the student can use one of their own cards to match any of the face-up cards on the table. If they are able to make a pair, they put those two cards to one side.
       Or the student can pick a card from the pile and try to match it with a card from their hand or from those face up on the table. If they are able to make a pair, they put those two cards to one side. If they can't make a pair, they must keep the card.
       Note that students may only make pairs from the Key vocabulary.
   ▸   Whenever a player makes a pair with one of the face-up cards on the table, they have to place one of their cards face up on the table, so that there is always the same number of cards face up on the table as there are players in the game.
   ▸   The first player to get rid of all their cards is the winner.

Variation

1   In groups of three to four, students shuffle the cards and lay them face down in front of them.
2   Players take turns to turn over any two cards. If the cards form a compound from the Key vocabulary, they may keep the cards and have another turn. If they do not form a compound from the Key vocabulary, they put the cards back in the same place, face down on the table.
3   The game continues until all the cards have been matched. The player with the most pairs is the winner.

Follow-up

In their groups, students take turns to pick a word from the envelope. They name the compound word associated with that word and talk for one minute on that subject, e.g. if they pick *battery*, they have to talk about *battery farming*.

Homework

A   Write ten sentences using compounds from the activity which you particularly want to remember.
B   Find other compounds which use one part of the words on the photocopiable page, e.g. *bottle opener*, *blood bank*.

greenhouse	effect	ozone	layer	traffic	jam
battery	farming	waste	disposal	drug	addiction
acid	rain	bottle	bank	global	warming
capital	punishment	oil	slick	road	rage
black	market	litter	bin	football	hooligan
welfare	state	animal	rights	shanty	town
water	shortage	blood	sports	sniffer	dog
power	cut	health	hazard	sexual	harassment

Thanks and acknowledgements

The authors and publishers would like to thank the following individuals for their help in commenting on the material, piloting it with their students and providing invaluable feedback:

Maria Heloisa Alves Aldino, Brazil

Ian Chitty, UK

Marie-Christine Cousin, France

Miles Craven, UK

Elisabeth de Lange, Germany

Gill Hamilton, Spain

Jan Isaksen, Mexico

Almut Koester, Germany

Patrick Lee, Hong Kong

Agnieszka Lenko-Szymanska, Poland

Kimberly Moss, UK

Barbara Nélaton, France

Mark O'Neil, Japan

Sue Wood, UK

Text design: Kamae Design, Oxford

Page make-up: Kamae Design, Oxford

Cover illustration: Jamel Akib

Illustrations: Kathy Baxendale (pp. 43, 47, 49, 51, 61, 97); Karen Donnelly (pp. 19, 67); Phil Healy (pp. 74); Steve Lach (pp. 23, 74); Nick Schon (pp. 11, 29, 53, 81); Lisa Smith (pp. 59, 91, 109); Sam Thompson (p. 95)